COLOUR
Fawn or brindle. White markings acceptable not exceeding one-third of ground colour.

GENERAL APPEARANCE
Great nobility, smooth-coated, medium-sized, square build, strong bone and evident, well developed muscles.

SIZE
Height: dogs 57-63 cms (22.5-25 ins); bitches 53-59 cms (21-23 ins).

TAIL
Set on high, customarily docked and carried upward.

HINDQUARTERS
Very strong with muscles hard and standing out noticeably under skin. Thighs curved and broad. Broad croup slightly sloped, with flat, broad arch.

COAT
Short, glossy, smooth and tight to body.

FEET
Front feet small and cat-like, with well arched toes, and hard pads; hind feet slightly longer.

Photo credits:

Norvia Behling
Carolina Biological Supply
Doskocil
Theresa Fico
Isabelle Francais
James Hayden-Yoav
James R. Hayden, RBP
Carol Ann Johnson
Dwight R. Kuhn
Dr. Dennis Kunkel

Jeff Michals
Mikki Pet Products
Alice Pantfoeder
Antonio Philippe
Phototake
Jean Claude Revy
Alice Roche
Paul Scott
Nikki Sussman
Alice van Kempen
C. James Webb

Printed in China.

The publisher is indebted to Richard Tomita for the submission of photographs for this book.

Illustrations by Renee Low

Copyright © 1999 Animalia, Ltd.

Cover patent pending.

PetLove™

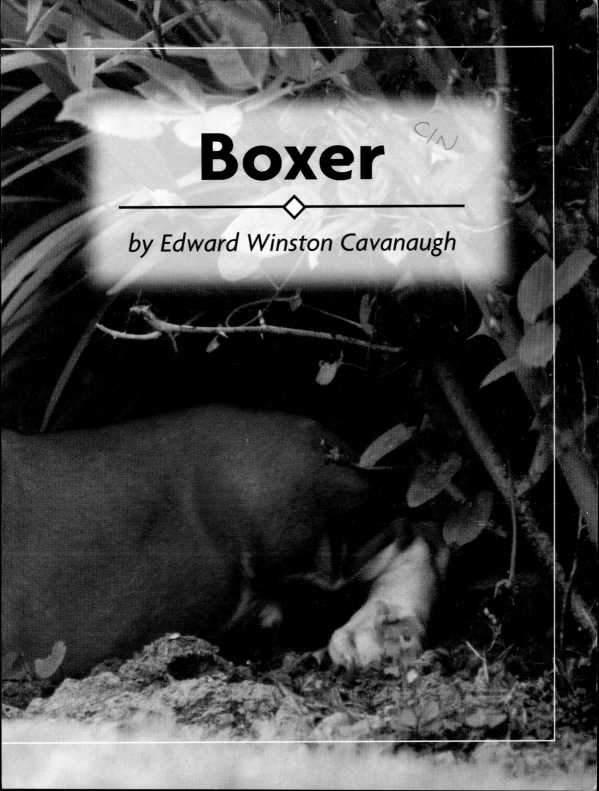

Boxer

◇

by Edward Winston Cavanaugh

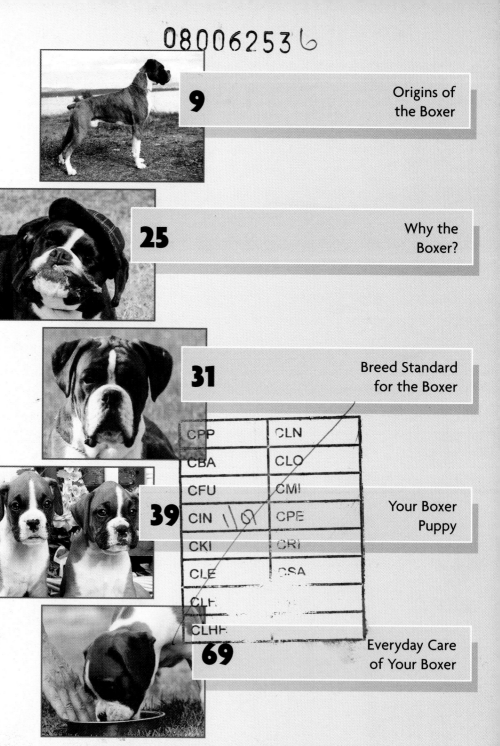

08006253 6

Table of Contents

Ancestors of the Boxer were originally trained and bred for hunting pigs, boar and deer. Less inclined to pursue wild game, today's Boxer is primarily a guard dog and house pet.

Origins of the Boxer

Most dog historians acknowledge that the Boxer derives from Bullenbeisser ancestry. These Bullenbeissers, or bull-biters, were hunting dogs, mostly used on pig, boar and deer. Such wild-game expeditions often cost the lives of many dogs, as the hunt was grue-some and gruelling for humans and dogs alike—not to mention the boars! Some sources say that these massive medieval dogs had erect ears and huge teeth, which would be used to hold the animal by the nose. It's probable that hunters were cropping ears the way they do in some countries today, since such a cruel custom would seem in tune with the primitive folk of the time period.

Not all generations of dogs have lived in civilised times like our own! It's always the contention of the living that our times are the

Int. Ch. Formula Miller of Norwegian and Canadian origin. Boxers of fine quality are available not only in Germany but also throughout the European continent and Great Britain.

Boxers were rarely, if ever, used for fighting as they were neither agile enough nor small enough to dodge bulls' attacks.

DID YOU KNOW?

It was only in the nineteenth century that humans really took notice of the dogs around them, and how they looked, what colour they were and how tall they were. Dogs all along have been helpmates—some dogs hunted, some killed vermin and some dogs protected property. No one bred the big black dog to the big black bitch because they were both black and big, necessarily. More than likely, humans paired dogs for their abilities. To produce a strong, protective dog, they would mate two dogs with those desirable qualities. Thus were progenerated various dogs with superior abilities.

were quicker and more inclined to fight 'head on.' These miniature gladiators (weighing approximately 35 to 55 pounds) would excel in the dog pit, battling fellow canines. The 'sport' of dog fighting followed swiftly on the heels of animal baiting. Dog fights became even more the bomb! In some countries today, including such civilised nations as

the U.S., such heinous sporting still goes on. By the mid-nineteenth century, bull baiting as well as dog fighting were banned by the German government.

On a more civilised and utilitarian route, the Boxer's ancestors were commonly employed as butcher dogs, for their ability to hold a bull and drive the animal

most civilised and acceptable of all times in history. The ancestors of our beloved Boxers did not have it so easy. They came about at a time when humans were obsessed with 'blood sports.' The baiting of bulls and bears was a mainstream attraction, and dogs that were strong, agile and fearless were needed to win and to keep the paying audience aroused. Fortunately for our friend the Boxer, his ancestors were not ideally suited for this bloody pastime: they were neither agile enough nor small enough to dodge the horns and hooves of the poor captive bull, which passionately was trying to protect itself from the jaws of the dogs. The smaller dogs

into its pen, should it become unruly. The famous reputation of the dog named 'Boxl', used by a butcher in Berlin, is credited for giving the 'breed' its name. The derivation of the word Boxer for a purebred dog is ironical, since the term 'boxl' or 'boxel' essentially translates to mutt! In 1894 a famous dog breeder of Bulldogs by the name of Friedrich Roberth was the first to coin the name 'Boxer' in print. His article which ran in a local paper complimented the Boxer for its intelligence and appearance, ranking the dog higher than any of the other breeds Roberth had owned, which were considerable. He acknowledged, however, that his Boxer bitch had a cleft palate and loose shoulder, but

otherwise was very impressive to all who met her. He also states that there were no breeders of the German Boxer who were pursuing a serious programme, adding that it was rare to get a litter with more than one or two good pups. Roberth's article concludes with a plea for any established, knowledgable dog person to initiate a club for the Boxer in Germany. As is the case in the dog world today, a new breed is best established by persons already 'in the fancy.' Roberth knew that this was the only viable way for a new breed to take hold in Germany.

Fortunately, the Germans, like the British, have never been slow to form a committee! And within one year of Roberth's plea, the Munich

The first dog show in which Boxers participated may well have been in Munich, Germany in 1895. Boxers have undergone serious changes since that time and today's Boxers are much more uniform in terms of size, structure and personality.

The expression of a good Boxer should be proud and alert.

Boxer Club was formed in 1895. At the first dog show that allowed Boxers (with an entry of four!), Flocki, owned by G. Muhlbauer of Munich, was the first Boxer to win a class. Roberth and a handful of fanciers began the German Boxer Club later that year, and Roberth was called upon to draft a standard for the breed. A standard is a written description of how an ideal specimen of the breed should appear; such a document, once endorsed by the club, becomes the measuring stick for breeders and judges. The first sentence of this early standard still perfectly describes our Boxer: 'The outward appearance should be of a compact, solid, sturdy, powerful and active dog that stands proudly and moves on straight healthy legs.'

This standard was based on the Boxer that was regarded as the best dog around. His name was Flock St. Salvador, and he won the first show

A standard is a measuring stick for breeders and judges.

for Boxers in 1896. The famous German Boxer magazine, *Der Boxer Blatter,* was established in 1904 and is still published today.

The dog that would become the most important stud dog in the

breed is Champion Rolf v. Vogelsberg, owned by Philip Stockmann, regarded as 'the father of the Boxer'. His wife, equally famous, was Friederun Miriam Stockmann, who continued to make their von Dom kennel famous after Philip's death. In World War One, the Boxer was fast chosen as a military dog and messenger dog. The Stockmanns provided many Boxers for the military, and the drafted Philip worked as a trainer for the services, leaving Frau Stockmann alone to handle their kennels. The War was claiming most usable Boxers for sentry and guard duty against snipers. Amongst the first dogs selected were the able and proven Boxer champions, given the breed's robustness and athletic ability. According to German Kennel Club regulations, the title of champion also required the dog to be of fit, working ability, so champions were the obvious first choice as they were already versed in Schutzhund or similar type obedience training. Many of the dogs that served in the military died in service, including hundreds of family pets. Rolf von Vogelsberg proved his worth as a war dog, and lived to tell about it (he also sired a couple of litters during the course of the war!). As a show dog, he was undefeated and secured five championships (the last of which was won after the war).

Shortly after the war, the Stockmanns' reputation for excellent Boxers was far-reaching, and

DID YOU KNOW?

Boxers have been used as military dogs since World War I. Their roles have been numerous. The dogs served as sentries, guards, mine detectors, rescuers of wounded soldiers and carriers of food and medicine.

many wealthy Americans sought German-bred Boxers to improve their breeding programmes. Frau Stockmann, who had endured many hardships with the War and had little money to keep her kennel running, was forced to sell some of her best dogs, not the least of

which was Ch. Sigurd von Dom, one of her most promising stud dogs, followed by the great Ch. Lustig von Dom, considered to be the most influential Boxer of all time. It was the Tulgey Wood Kennels in America that purchased Lustig, and this line would eventually yield the greatest show dog of all time, Ch. Bang Away of Sirrah Crest, a dog that is still referred to today as the ultimate Boxer.

The Second World War reduced Frau Stockmann to desperate measures, even though her Boxers were amongst the dogs deemed worthy to be fed. The German government designated which breeds, based on their utility, were cost-effective to sustain. The Boxer was the number-

The early German Boxers in the 1900s were characterised by this famous photo of Dr. Grete Maria Ehrenstein, a famous Viennese beauty. Note that the dogs' ears were cropped even then!

The German Boxer of 1903 showed similarities to the French Bulldog and the Boston Terrier even though direct ancestral proof is elusive.

The German Boxer was used for bull-baiting, the same as the British Bulldog, in the 1890s.

The German Boxer of 1905 showed more prominent Boston Terrier features than modern Boxers display.

two breed selected, on the heels of the German Shepherd Dog. Frau Stockmann trained dogs for messenger service, which required that the dogs perform under the 'distraction' of gunfire. The Boxer proved particular adept, not surprisingly. American troops stationed in Germany greatly admired the Boxer, and many drab-green passers-by told the Frau that the Boxer was the number-one breed in America. Frau Stockmann relished hearing about the Boxer's popularity in America, knowing that her beloved breed would continue worldwide years after she was gone.

What Is Schutzhund?

In the German language, Schutzhund translates to 'protection dog.' Many of the working dogs of Germany, the Boxer, Dobermann, Rottweiler and German Shepherd Dog, are trained in Schutzhund. Developed at the turn of the 20th century, Schutzhund includes not only protection training but also tracking and obedience. One of the principles of Schutzhund is that dogs must bark before they bite, and they are taught to seize and hold an opponent without actually tearing his limbs apart. Protection training for dogs utilises a sleeve that the dog is taught to grasp and hold.

A few years later, Frau Stockmann was invited to the United States, where she judged the breed and was gifted with dogs by some of America's top breeders. While in the States, she also had the opportunity to judge the three-month-old Bang Away of Sirrah Crest. She awarded him Best Puppy in Match, over 110 puppies, and referred to him as 'Little Lustig.' Her eye for a dog was never more precise, as Bang Away would go on to earn a record-breaking 121 Best in Show awards, including the famous Westminster Kennel Club.

THE BOXER IN THE UNITED KINGDOM

Philip Stockmann, the famous German breeder of Boxers, fretted over the breed's name in his book *My Life with Boxers*. He bemoaned that this valiant German dog has an English name! The Boxer, we must admit, does have ties to the United Kingdom, and there's more than a little Bulldog in the Boxer's blood.

The first imported Boxer arrived in Britain in 1933, when it was registered with The Kennel Club. In 1939, the first champion was recorded: Ch. Horsa of Leith Hill, bred by Mrs. D. Sprig, the first secretary of the British Boxer Club, which was founded three years earlier in 1936. Despite Horsa's accomplishment, he would have no lasting influence on the Boxer breed in England, as the breed remained in relative obscurity until after the Second World War.

A lovely modern British Boxer shows off his typical flashy markings.

15

From 1936 to 1953, Allon Dawson of the Stainburndorf prefix imported many Boxers into Britain from Germany, Holland and the U.S., the most important of which was Ch. Zunftig von Dom, son of Lustig, bred by the Stockmanns. Although Zunftig was in England only a short time before being sent to the U.S., he was able to sire the great Zulu, who was to become a profound influence on the British Boxer. Another fabulous German import

Solid-coloured fawn dogs are less favoured than flashier dogs.

from the Stockmanns was Frohlich von Dom, at the time considered the best import from Germany. From America, Dawson received excellent dogs from Mazelaine and Sirrah Crest, two of the most influential kennels in the States.

Panfield Serenade, owned by Elizabeth Montgomery-Somerfield, was the first bitch champion with The Kennel Club. Serenade was the granddaughter to Lustig. Pat Withers of the Witherford prefix also produced marvellous show dogs, including a line of four generations of champions. Her most famous dog is Int. Ch. Witherford's Hot Chestnut, who goes back to

Collo von Dom, bred by Frau Stockmann. No matter which country you visit, the von Dom kennel influence is always present, a lasting tribute to the great Frau Stockmann.

The American influence on the Boxer in Britain can be traced to the country's respect for John P. Wagner, who visited England in the 1950s. Wagner was the proprietor of the famed Mazelaine Kennels, one of the largest Boxer establishments ever. The 'flashiness' of the Boxer, ignited by the white blaze on the head, chest and feet, is associated with many famous American show dogs. The solid-coloured fawn dogs, exemplary of the English Boxer tradition, were losing favour to the flashier American type. Ch. Seefeld's Picasso, bred by Pat Heath, is a fine example of a flashy Boxer who won grandly in the U.K. (acquiring some 24 Challenge Certificates). Amongst other pioneers that paraded flashy Boxers was Charles Walker of the Lynpine Kennels, whose dogs trace back to Hot Chestnut (and therefore Frau Stockmann). Walker also introduced many great Dutch Boxers into his British bloodlines. The Newlaithe Boxers, owned by Christine and Patrick Beardsell, trace back to Frohlich von Dom. This kennel has also imported some flashy American Boxers from Richard Tomita of the Jacquet Kennels.

The typical high-quality British Boxer looks more like the American Boxer than the older British dog.

Pet owners still want a Boxer that looks like a Boxer. Consider all the points in the standard when selecting a Boxer, even if you're not purchasing a dog to show.

ABC in the USA

The American Boxer Club, Inc., known as the ABC, has held a national speciality every year since 1936. The early years of the Boxer fancy in the U.S. was dominated by great German imports, and the first winner of the speciality was Ch. Corso v. Uracher Wasserfall Se Sumbula, bred by Karl Walz of Germany. Entries at the first shows only drew around 50 dogs to compete; in time the show would attract over 400 Boxers. Compared to numbers at The Kennel Club's shows, these numbers are fairly insubstantial, but given the geographic size of the U.S., these numbers represent only the dogs able to travel the distance to the show, which is held every year in the Northeast.

BOXERS IN THE UNITED STATES AND AROUND THE WORLD

The Boxer, whose humble beginnings in Germany as a 'mongrel' boar hunter, would rise to great fame around the world, not the least of which was in the U.S. American breeders have had significant influence on the breed in many countries, with many imports sent to establish new bloodlines and to set the type of the 'definitive show Boxer'. The American dog scene has never recovered from the explosion of Bang Away in the 1950s. This likeable showman of a Boxer was featured on the cover of dog magazines and sports magazines alike! He paved the way for other show dogs to pursue astronomical records in the ring. Although Bang Away's record of 121 Bests in Shows has been topped by many great show dogs in this day of modern travel and red-hot competition in the dog world, it has still not been topped by a Boxer! When Bang Away won the Westminster Kennel Club show in Madison Square Garden in 1951, the breed was the top dog in registrations with the American Kennel Club. (Today the Boxer ranks in the top twenty, but rarely higher than ten.) Bang Away's Boxer predecessor as Westminster victor was Ch. Warlord of Mazelaine, bred by John P. Wagner and owned by Mr. and Mrs. Richard Kettles; his successor for the crown was Ch. Arriba's Prima Donna, bred by Theodore S. Fickes, DVM.

The American Boxer Club (ABC) was established in 1936, the

DID YOU KNOW?
The Boxer has been used in more areas of service to humankind than almost any other breed. Here are ten important areas that the breed has served:
1. Wartime and military work.
2. Police assitance and demonstrations.
3. Guides for the blind.
4. Hearing dogs for the deaf.
5. Arson and bomb detection.
6. Drug and substance detection.
7. Guard dogs for businesses and residences.
8. Search and rescue/avalanche and earthquake work.
9. Therapy dogs for hospitals.
10. Cancer detection.

Boxers can make friends with anyone—even this strange long-eared fellow!

same year that the Germans first organised their club. The ABC held its first specialty show that same year and it was won by Ch. Corso v. Uracher Wasserfall se Sumbula, bred by Karl Walz of Germany. Amongst the breed greats to win this Boxer showdown were Ch. Warlord of Mazelaine, Ch. Bang Away of Sirrah Crest, who both also won WKC, Ch. Baroque of Quality Hill, Ch. Treceder's Painted Lady, Ch. Salgray's Fashion Plate, Ch. Arriba's Prima Donna, also a WKC BIS winner, Ch. Scher-Khoun Shadrack of the famous Canadian kennel owned by Ben de Boer, Ch. Wagner Wilverday Famous Amos, a four-time victor, and Ch. Kiebla's Tradition of Tu-Ro, a three-time victor (and three-time runner up as Best of Opposite Sex).This list of greats fairly represents the best breeding in the U.S. and the progeny of these great dogs produced magnificently in the States and elsewhere.

Many prominent British kennels have imported Boxers from American breeders in an effort to give their dogs more flash and substance.

The Boxer in Canada was first recognised in 1934, and the first registered dog was Anthony Adverse of Barmere, owned by Marion Young (Breed), who purchased Sigurd von Dom from Frau Stockmann. The American dog scene has always had great impact on the Canadian dog world, given the size of the U.S., its proximity and the open border between the two nations. Amongst the pioneer Canadian kennels we have Quality, Allison, Blossomlea, Haviland, and Malabar. The Boxer Club of Canada was formed in 1947, after the first club, the Western Boxer Club, disbanded the previous year. Amongst the nation's most famous Boxers is Int. Ch. Millan's Fashion Hint, out of Salgray bloodlines, who sired over 100 champions, including his world-renowned son Int. Ch. Scher-Khoun's Shadrack, also the sire of over 100 champions. Fashion Hint was bred and owned by Michael Millan. Amongst the top-producing kennels in Canada we have Ajay, Bellcrest, Blossomlea, Chardepado, Diamondaire, Fisher, Gaylord, Glencotta, Golden Haze, Haviland, Jaegerhouse, Memorylane, Mephisto, Millan, Pinepath, Rodonna, Scher-Khoun, Shadowdale, Starview, Trimanor, and Verwood, each of which has produced no fewer than 20 champions each. Leading this prestigious pack is Haviland, which has produced about three times more than any other, totalling over 150 champions.

In this humorous photo, the Boxer's similarity to an English Bulldog is unmistakable.

In Holland, the Boxer scene is lead off by Piet van Melis, whose observations about England and the Continent are valuable: 'In England, there is far less difference between the dogs because judges and breeders are looking more for the overall quality of the dog. In European countries, the head of the Boxer is of the highest importance, then comes the body, and movement is the last to be looked at.' Despite Germany's stronghold on the Boxer breed, Holland has produced many excellent dogs, not the least of which is Mr. van Melis's Int. Ch. Casper van Worikben.

Despite the Germans' influence and predominance in the European Boxer world, the extremely independent Dutchmen wanted little to do with the Germans after the Second World

War and they discontinued use of the German lines. Over the years, the Dutch developed a distinctive Boxer that is heavy, strong and round, short-coated, with a superb head, not too short, and proportionate to the body.

In Germany the Boxer must pass difficult tests in order to be considered a champion. These tests concern health, type and character. The first is an elementary test known as ZVP (which is very short for *Zuchtveranlangungsprufung*),

German Boxer pedigrees often contain test results as suffixes attached to the dogs' names.

which includes a check for 'normal' or better hips. Additionally a dog must pass three levels of Schutzhund tests and three levels of the IPO, and the test called *Ankorung*, a difficult test for type, quality and character, which is repeated every two years. German pedigrees list the results of these tests so that breeders can thoroughly and effectively evaluate the ancestry of the dogs (in terms of character, type and health). Unlike in the U.S. and England where a pedigree merely lists the names of the dogs in the ancestry (and

whether or not they were champions), pedigrees in Germany give breeders insight into all the areas of importance to determining whether or not to breed to a certain dog. Fortunately for the international Boxer scene, more and more kennel clubs are encouraging this type of documentation on the dogs.

The first American Boxer to be imported into Japan was sent in 1957 from the Mazelaine kennels, who was followed shortly by Ch. Canzonet's Minute-Minder, whose progeny dominated Japan in the 1960s. The American influence on Japan can hardly be overstated. Mazelaine sold some of their best dogs to Japan, including two ABC Best in Show winners. One of the most prominent Japanese Boxer breeders, Dr. Hideaki Nakazawa, also a popular judge in the U.S., has imported many great Boxers from the States, including Int. Ch. Jacquet's Urko from Richard Tomita's famous kennel in New Jersey. Three other Jacquet Boxers followed, including the world-renowned International Champion Novarese, and the Jacquet-style dog—strong, flashy, dramatic—began to dominate Japan. The Jacquet Boxers have 'invaded' many other countries other than Japan, though given breeder Richard Tomita's Japanese ancestry, it's no wonder he has so generously shared his

The Scandinavian Norwegian Swedish Ch. Larun Your Choice was bred from champion dogs in Norway and Finland.

One of the most gorgeous Boxer heads in the world is held proud by the famous Spanish champion Janos de Loermo of Lynpine.

dogs with his parents' homeland. Among the other countries that Jacquet has profoundly influenced are Argentina, Australia, Brazil, Canada, India, Japan, the Philippines, Taiwan and Mexico. In his monumental volume *The World of the Boxer*, Richard Tomita modestly pens, 'I am happy to see Jacquet has helped to build the foundation for many lines and kennels throughout the world...I am grateful to the devoted Boxer fanciers and breeders who have guided me with their knowledge or their strong lines that they have produced so that I was able to further this wondrous world of the Boxer.'

23

Many dog lovers buy champion-quality Boxers just for the sheer joy of showing (and winning) at local competitions.

Why the Boxer?

IS THE BOXER THE RIGHT DOG FOR YOU?

Let's face it. Our Boxer today has very little to do with the bull-biting matador of yesteryear. This author is certain that your reason for considering a Boxer is not to hold a hog down while you tie and spit it. Although it's fascinating to learn about the origins of our beloved Boxer, few of us today can relate to those butcher-dog legends. We can imagine, however, that the dog used to pin a wild boar to the forest floor needed courage, stamina and determination. These are three desirable qualities for a protection dog, which the Boxer delivers today in full force. I am not certain that the breed's original function required very much intelligence on the part of the dogs. It doesn't seem that an overly intelligent animal could fancy the gory, mindless work of the early Boxers. Nonetheless, the breed today has overcome this primitive mentality and is a resourceful, intelligent dog.

There are many endearing qualities that characterise the Boxer breed. He is sweet, good-humoured, family-oriented, trainable and adaptable. The temperament of the Boxer cannot be compromised. Of all the working dogs, the Boxer stands out for the

Prospective owners selecting their house pet. By definition, the Boxer is sweet and family-oriented, thriving on the attention of people.

sweetness of his character. A mean Boxer is an oxymoron: no such animal should exist. Boxers are people dogs, devoutly attached to their families and protective. Today's Boxer is indeed a stylish companion dog as well as a guardian. This is a handsome dog who cuts a unique silhouette in dogdom. Standing proudly in the centre ring at a dog show or in the middle of your garden or parlour, the Boxer impresses all those who rest eyes upon him.

Within a family a Boxer thrives best. He is gentle with children, respectful of the elderly, and obedient to each family member. Boxers recognise friends instinctively. Unlike less discriminating dogs, such as the Golden Retriever and Beagle, the Boxer does not accept everyone as his 'best chum'. When your Boxer backs away from an individual or growls, he is telling you that there is something not quite right in the air. Boxers are tremendously good character judges. I have known more than one married couple who considered separating because the new Boxer decided one or the other wasn't 'up to snuff.' Perhaps that's taking the Boxer's instincts too far—they are instinctive not psychic!

Do dogs get any cuter than this one? If you fall in love with a Boxer puppy, your expressions of attachment are a healthy part of dog-human bonding.

To say that the Boxer is train-able is not to say that he is easily trained. A dedicated owner, who understands the way a Boxer thinks, will have very few prob-lems training the Boxer. Unlike his ancestors, Boxers tend to ask 'why' before they execute a com-mand. Especially before they exe-cute a command four or five times simultaneously. Boxers tend to be too smart for their own good. This author has never read any leg-endary account of a medieval Boxer that refused to grab its fif-teenth boar by the nose. Today's more modern-thinking Boxers need a bit more prodding to exe-cute obedience work. That there are hundreds of obedience-titled Boxers around us, not to mention highly trained service dogs, police dogs and military dogs, speaks well for the trainability of the Boxer. All these occupations also convince one of the adaptability of the Boxer, able to live in practi-cally any situation with a family, a couple or just an individual.

Since Boxers are so people-orient-ed, they care very little about their living environment. A Boxer can dwell contentedly in a small flat with a terrace or garden, as long as he get attention and adequate exercise. Similarly the Boxer is content on a grand estate with a large fenced-in property. He will guard both homes, and his own-ers, with his whole spirit and his whole heart.

Boxers are famous for the ability to judge character. If they love you, they show it!

Though Boxers were never trained as water dogs, many of them do have an attraction to water.

Despite their warm, loveable nature, Boxers can immediately become fearless guard dogs.

Every Boxer's favourite holiday is Valentine's Day! Not just because this winter holiday is a great cause to warm up, but because it's about love and kissing. Boxers are great kissers—just ask a Boxer owner! Many breeders will confess that the Boxer is all bark. Once you get close to a group of vociferous Boxers, spewing and spitting as they announce their warning, they will lick you to death! That's not to suggest that the Boxer is incapable of defending his home. I have been astonished (repeatedly) every time one of my sweet loving Boxers sud-

denly turned ferocious at the sound of something threatening or ominous. Despite all the kissing and cooing, the Boxer is still a fearless guard dog. But still in all, he's more of a lover than a fighter!

Many people contend that a Boxer is a breed that you keep for life. Many of today's Boxer owners grew up with a Boxer or remember being strongly imprinted upon by a Boxer (perhaps an uncle or neighbour had an outstanding dog). Having grown up with a Boxer often convinces adults to share a Boxer with their own children. On the other hand, many households without children adopt Boxers because they are described as intelligent as a seven-year-old child, and surely more obedient! Then there are those 'grown-up' parents, whose children have moved out of the

DID YOU KNOW?

You have never known love like the love of a Boxer. While the love of dogs is well known, the Boxer goes beyond the bounds of an owner's expectations. In a recent book by Jeffrey Moussaieff Masson, *Dogs Never Lie About Love*, he quotes Fritz von Unruh: 'The dog is the only being that loves you more than you love yourself.' I would bet that Fritz was a Boxer owner! Perhaps it is this love of humankind that has inspired the greater intelligence of our Boxers, the sweetness of temperament, and the total trustworthiness of the Boxer breed. It is completely in harmony with modern-day thinking that such emotion could generate critical qualities in our companion animals.

household, who adopt a Boxer for their golden years. As Boxer people will reveal, a home is not a home without a Boxer.

The Boxer has proven its worth to humankind by performing in various service capacities. In addition to its role in the military, the Boxer has donned a badge as a police dog, assisting the legal forces of many nations. In homes, the Boxer's steady temperament and affinity for the human touch have made the breed a superior choice for PAT dogs and therapy dogs. Whether the Boxer's ears flop naturally or stand erect, it is first and foremost a 'hearing' dog. The AKC standard describes the Boxer as a 'hearing guard dog,' thus also making him a definitive choice for the deaf. Other physically challenged individuals rely on

DID YOU KNOW?
When searching for a Boxer, owners are well advised to not seek out dogs that are bigger than the standard describes. These dogs will more likely suffer from joint problems and other conditions that accompany overbreeding and oversized dogs.

Boxers as well, including those confined to a wheelchair and the blind, for whom the Boxer serves as a Seeing Eye™ dog or guide dog. Not only does the Boxer offer his ears and eyes to humankind, he also offers his nose! As a search and rescue dog, the Boxer has assisted rescue workers in emergencies, such as earthquakes and avalanches. The Boxer is able to 'sniff' out lost individuals buried under knee-deep snow, rock or rubble.

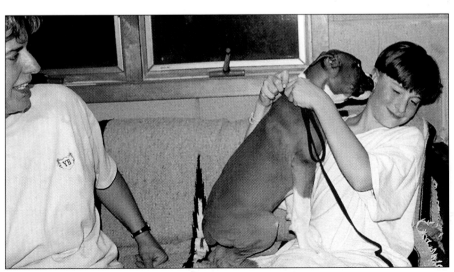

Boxers are kissers; they are lovers, not fighters!

29

Boxers are not only handsome dogs but also dependable pets and guardians. Most Boxers are easily trainable as well.

Breed Standard
for the Boxer

Definition: A standard is a written description of what the ideal representative of a breed should look like.

A standard is drafted by a breed club, like the British Boxer Club or the German Boxer Club, and then submitted for acceptance to the national kennel club. The Kennel Club controls all standards for the

U.K. Breeders and other experts usually convene to put the ineffable perfect dog into words. Composing such a word picture is fraught with difficulty and dissension, since words are prone to interpretation and the meaning of words vary. For instance, if a dog's muzzle is described as 'broad and deep', just how broad and how deep should

the perfect muzzle be. What is in balance to one viewer is totally out of balance to the next. Thus, breeders could never agree on the perfect dog even if it walked into the show ring! Nonetheless, the breed standard is the best measuring stick available for determining which Boxers are excellent and which are below-average. The Boxer standard, as accepted by The Kennel Club, has many sections that are very specific. Study the section Head and Skull carefully. There is no doubt that the British fanciers revere the Boxer's head, and the detail set forth in the standard on the head does not leave too much room for poor interpretation. The standard is used by judges in the show ring, just as breeders use the standard to decide which dogs are worth breeding and which dogs are not.

The standard included here is approved by The Kennel Club, the leading dog-governing body of the U.K. On the Continent, as well as in the U.S. and elsewhere, standards vary considerably, in both wording and content. A dog deemed of inferior quality in Great Britain can be exported to the U.S. or Denmark, for example, and be selected Best in Show. The reverse is true too,

Boxer champions are magnificent animals. The standard describes the ideal Boxer.

The Boxer

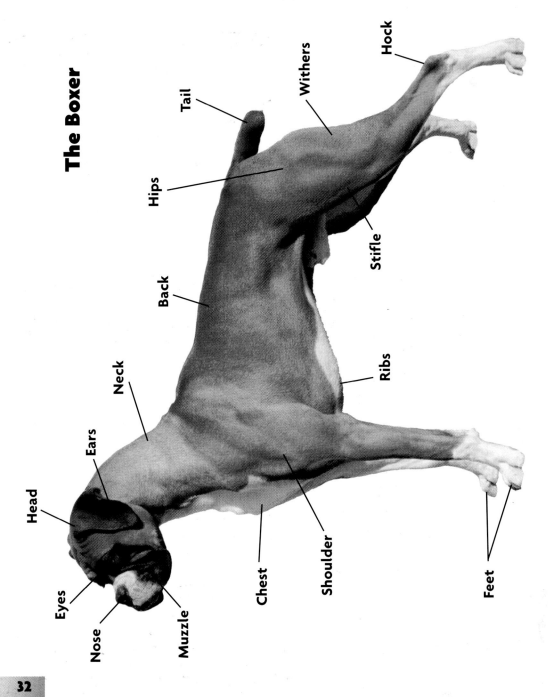

Head

Ears

Neck

Eyes

Nose

Muzzle

Chest

Shoulder

Feet

Back

Hips

Tail

Withers

Hock

Stifle

Ribs

though the British system is much more rigorous than any other kennel club in the world. Most judiciary systems require that at least three different judges recommend the dog for top honours before it can be called a champion. This requirement theoretically diminishes the subjective nature of judging and interpreting the breed standard.

The muzzle must be broad, deep and powerful.

THE KENNEL CLUB STANDARD FOR THE BOXER

General Appearance: Great nobility, smooth-coated, medium-sized, square build, strong bone and evident, well developed muscles.

Characteristics: Lively, strong, loyal to owner and family, but distrustful of strangers. Obedient, friendly at play, but with guarding instinct.

Temperament: Equable, biddable, fearless, self-assured.

Head and Skull: Head imparts its unique individual stamp and is in proportion to body, appearing neither light nor too heavy. Skull lean without exaggerated cheek muscles. Muzzle broad, deep and powerful, never narrow, pointed, short or shallow. Balance of skull and muzzle essential, with muzzle never appearing small, viewed from any angle. Skull cleanly covered, showing no wrinkle, except when alerted. Creases present from root of nose running down sides of muzzle. Dark mask confined to muzzle, distinctly contrasting with colour of head, even when white is present. Lower jaw undershot, curving slightly upward. Upper jaw broad where attached to skull, tapering very slightly to front. Muzzle shape complete by upper lips, thick and well padded, supported by well sep-

The Boxer's head imparts its unique stamp on the breed, bearing an intelligent and friendly expression.

arated canine teeth of lower jaw. Lower edge of upper lip rests on edge of lower lip, so that chin is clearly perceptible when viewed from front or side. Lower jaw never to obscure front of upper lip, neither should teeth nor tongue be visible when mouth closed. Top of skull slightly arched, not rounded, nor too flat and broad. Occiput not too pronounced. Distinct stop, bridge of nose never forced back into forehead, nor should it be downfaced. Length of muzzle measured from tip of nose to inside corner of eye is one-third length of head measured from tip of nose to occiput. Nose broad, black, slightly turned up, wide nostrils with well defined line between. Tip of nose set slightly higher than root of muzzle. Cheeks powerfully developed, never bulging.

Eyes: Dark brown, forward looking, not too small, protruding or deeply set. Showing lively, intelligent expression. Dark rims with good pigmentation showing no haw.

Ears: Moderate size, thin, set wide apart on highest part of skull lying flat and close to cheek in repose, but falling forward with definite crease when alert.

The body must have a square profile.

Mouth: Undershot jaw, canines set wide apart with incisors (six) in straight line in lower jaw. In upper jaw set in line curving slightly forward. Bite powerful and sound, with teeth set in normal arrangement.

Neck: Round, of ample length, strong, muscular, clean cut, no dewlap. Distinctly marked nape and elegant arch down to withers.

Forequarters: Shoulders long and sloping, close lying, not excessively covered with muscle. Upper arm long, making right angle to shoulderblade. Forelegs seen from front, straight, parallel, with strong bone. Elbows not too close or standing too far from chest wall. Forearms perpendicular, long and firmly muscled. Pasterns short, clearly defined, but not distended, slightly slanted.

Body: In profile square, length from forechest to rear of upper thigh equal to height at withers. Chest deep, reaching to elbows. Depth of chest half height at withers. Ribs well arched, not barrel-shaped, extending well to rear. Withers clearly defined. Back short, straight, slightly sloping , broad and strongly muscled. Loin short, well tucked up and taut. Lower abdominal line blends into curve to rear.

Champion Boxers should look and act with dignity and pride, just like this British show dog.

Hindquarters: Very strong with muscles hard and standing out noticeably under skin. Thighs broad and curved. Broad croup slightly sloped, with flat, broad arch. Pelvis long and broad. Upper and lower thigh long. Good hind angulation; when standing, the stifle is directly under the hip protuberance. Seen from side, leg from hock joint to foot not quite vertical. Seen from behind, legs straight, hock joints clean, with powerful rear pads.

Feet: Front feet small and cat-like, with well arched toes, and hard pads; hind feet slightly longer.

Tail: Set on high, customarily docked and carried upward.

Gait/Movement: Strong, powerful with noble bearing, reaching well forward, and with driving action of hindquarters. In profile, stride free and ground covering.

The judge's interpretation of the breed standard will determine whether or not your Boxer takes home a ribbon.

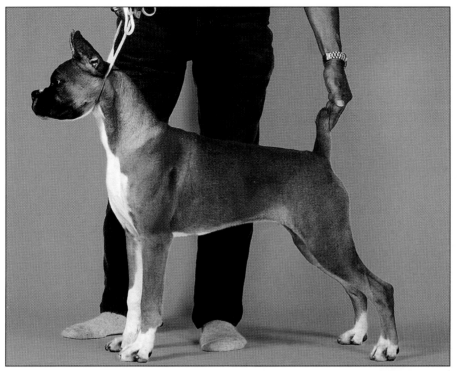

The American breed standard differs from the British standard significantly. The most dramatic departure concerns the cropping of the ears.

Coat: Short, glossy, smooth and tight to body.

Colour: Fawn or brindle. White markings acceptable not exceeding one-third of ground colour.

Fawn: Various shades from dark deer red to light fawn. Brindle: Black stripes on previously described fawn shades, running parallel to ribs all over body. Stripes contrast distinctly to ground colour, neither too close nor too thinly dispersed. Ground colour clear, not intermingling with stripes.

Size: Height: dogs: 57–63 cms (22.5–25 ins); bitches: 53–59 cms (21–23 ins). Weight: dogs: approximately 25–27 kgs (55–60 lbs).

Faults: Any departure from the foregoing points should be considered a fault and the seriousness with which the fault should be regarded should be in exact proportion to its degree.

Note: Male animals should have two apparently normal testicles fully descended into the scrotum.

37

EARS

Natural drop ears give the Boxer an intelligent and trustworthy expression. Cropped ears are disqualified in England.

HINDQUARTERS

The hindlegs should be straight, without weak or cowhocks.

FOREQUARTERS

Forequarters should be parallel, straight, never turning in or out at the elbows.

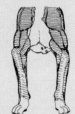

BACK

Back should be short and straight, never roached or sloping in topline.

GAIT

The Boxer gaits with strong driving action from the rear. In profile, he strides free and covers much ground.

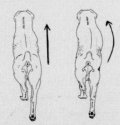

Your Boxer Puppy

OWNER CONSIDERATIONS
Any admirer of the Boxer can tell that he is a proud and confident dog. This 'purebred' certainty goes without saying—it's evident in the Boxer's carriage, his expression and his distinctive personality. But a Boxer is also a sensitive creature that depends on human interaction. This is a vital part of what makes a Boxer a Boxer. Boxers thrive on people, revelling in the licking and kissing of their family, and often quite eager to 'taste' any willing visitor. If you are looking for a dog that will sit handsomely on your mantle and never bother you, the Boxer is not the dog for you. If, however, you are willing to devote the time and attention to a Boxer that he rightly deserves, this is a breed for you for life!

Although the reader of these pages is more likely interested in finding a companionable and family animal than a show champion, there remain many serious factors governing your choice. A primary consideration is time, not only the time of the animal's allotted life span, which is over ten years, but also of the time required for the owner to exercise and care for the creature. If you are not committed to the welfare and whole existence of this energetic, purposeful animal; if, in the simplest, most basic example, you are not willing to walk

A proper breeder would not sell a puppy to people who would not or could not care for the Boxer puppy in a safe and humane manner.

your dog daily, despite the weather, do not choose a Boxer as a companion.

Space is another important consideration. The Boxer in early puppyhood may be well accommodated in a corner of your kitchen but after only six months when the dog is likely over 40 pounds, larger space certainly will be required. A garden with a fence is also a basic and reasonable expectation. Fortunately, most Boxers do not stray far from their properties (unless attracted

sure that you want a Boxer in your home and in your life.

Remember too that Boxer puppies can be very inventive, that is to say, destructive. Unless you can supervise a puppy 24 hours per day, you must expect that he's going to investigate and taste your woodwork, furniture, cabinets, etc. You must be prepared (emotionally and financially) for such mishaps. Needless to say, proper training and a dash of discipline are all it takes to correct such problems. If you are extremely fussy about your house and cannot tolerate muddy paws and slobbery jowls, go for a guppy or budgerigar and spare a Boxer the disappointment.

Likewise potential owners must consider that a dog

by a strong-scented bitch). Unlike other breeds that tend to 'escape' on a regular basis, the Boxer will not abandon his post. The fence is a convenient detail because it keeps strangers from wandering upon your property and challenging your Boxer.

A Boxer is not an outdoor dog. He wants to be as close to you as possible. He is not appropriately 'dressed' to spend all his days outside. He needs to be indoors with the family. A Boxer that is kept outdoors exclusively is a miserable dog. Don't subject your dog to such a life. Boxers do not tend to be independent and they want to follow you, spend time with you, sit with you, etc. Make

Boxers are prone to genetic diseases. Buy a healthy puppy and have it examined by a veterinary surgeon as soon as you buy it.

Try to observe your prospective Boxer puppy with its dam. If the dam plays with the puppies, you can take delight in knowing you will probably buy a puppy with an inherited friendly attitude.

impedes upon your freedom! You can no longer escape for a long weekend without preparing for your Boxer's accommodation. Perhaps you will choose a holiday that is suitable for a dog to come along, but the Boxer must now figure into your planning. Once you have selected a Boxer, and you have bonded with him, you will realise that you have found the ideal companion, one who accepts you for all your faults and appreciates every little thing you do for him! The Boxer's life expectancy is a sure ten years, perhaps even a few years longer. Since 10 to 12 years is a long expanse of time, you must commit to keeping the Boxer for his whole life. Many Boxers are success-

fully rehomed (placed in second homes) through rescue groups. Fortunately the Boxer's adaptability makes this unfortunate, heartbreaking situation more bearable. It's possible that you might want to consider adopting a Boxer from a rescue service. Since adopting an adult dog is almost always easier than

It is difficult to judge a puppy's personality until he is at least four weeks old.

A Boxer is not an outside dog. He wants to be as close to you as possible—that's why it is so easy to train him to heel.

starting from scratch (and bite) with a puppy, this is a sensible, viable option for many. If you would like to give a deserving Boxer a second chance, contact your local breed club or The Kennel Club for the appropriate source.

ACQUIRING A BOXER PUPPY
Due to the popularity of the Boxer, there are many reputable breeders to choose from, and there are even more breeders to avoid. You should seek out the best Boxer that you can afford. There is no such thing as 'just a pet dog' or a 'pet-quality dog'. You cannot afford to own a second-rate dog. Inferior quality in a pet only translates to high veterinary bills, wasted time, and broken hearts! You are seeking a Boxer that looks like a Boxer. You want your neighbours to admire your canine charge and tell you how handsome he is. If

If you buy a Boxer puppy, you must accept the responsibilities of ownership for at least ten years. Boxers usually live for over a decade.

the appearance of the dog doesn't matter, why get a Boxer? It's not that simple. You want a handsome Boxer that is the picture of good health: a pedigree that indicates his parents have normal or better hips, no history of cancers or the like in their backgrounds, and good eyes. Since the Boxer is prone to a number of genetic problems, you want the healthiest dog you can find. You're not merely investing money in this purchase—you're investing your heart and your family! What could be more costly than that? If the breeder is trying to pitch a 'pet-quality puppy' at you, tell him that you want the best puppy he has. While the conformation of the dog isn't a primary consideration for a pet person, all of the other important factors that breeders emphasize are. Reread the temperament and character portion of the breed standard: is there a single quality listed there that doesn't appeal to you?

Be aware that the novice breeders who advertise at attractive prices in the local newspapers are probably kind enough towards their dogs, but do not have the expertise or facilities required to raise these dogs properly. These pet puppies are frequently badly weaned and left with the mother too long without the supplemental feeding required by this fast-growing breed. This lack of proper feeding can cause indigestion, rickets, weak bones, poor teeth and other problems. Veterinary bills may soon distort initial savings into financial, or worse, emotional loss. Inquire about inoculations and when the puppy was last dosed for worms. Check the ears for signs of debris or irritation, indicating the presence of mites.

Boxers love people. Though loyal and protective when you are around, they will easily acclimate to a new home and new ownership should you be permanently separated.

DID YOU KNOW?
The puppy should have regular play and exercise sessions when he is with you or a family member. Exercise for a very young puppy can consist of a short walk around the house or garden. Playing can include fetching games with a large ball or an old sock with a knot tied in the middle. (All puppies teethe and need soft things upon which to chew.) Remember to restrict play periods to indoors within his living area (the family room, for example) until he is completely housetrained.

Colour is a matter of personal choice, but whether you prefer a bright fawn Boxer with flashy white markings or a brindle dog, your puppy should have a dark nose and, preferably, dark toenails. This is a consideration of pigmentation, which should not be confused with colour. Colour in Boxers generally becomes lighter, so it is wise to choose a puppy with deep rich pigmentation and as much black as possible. By six to ten weeks of age, the Boxer's nose should be well pigmented and broad. You do not want a Boxer puppy with a narrow nose, since its muzzle will likely not develop to the desired broadness. In selecting a fawn-coloured dog, seek a deep red colouration, especially down

43

This Boxer puppy's colour is not acceptable for a show dog, but as a pet dog the colour is enchanting.

These puppies are more traditionally coloured than the almost all-white puppy in the adjoining photo.

the back and head; in a brindle dog, look for distinctive herring-bone striations against a deep red background. For the flashy look, white markings should be present on the chest, legs, and the forehead and muzzle.

In show dogs, breeders seek out deep pigmentation comple-mented by white markings on the head, legs and chest. Dark eyes are best, and Boxer pups tend to have bluish eyes that darken as they age. Look for expression in your puppy's eyes, as this is a good sign of intelligence. Boxers often show the haw of the eye, one or both of which may be white; this adds to the Boxer expression. Since the Boxer is a 'head breed', you want a puppy that makes a pleasing impression. The Boxer puppy's muzzle

should be broad and deep; this is important for the expression of the dog as an adult. The puppy's head should have some wrinkles, which will disappear as the dog matures. Check that the puppy's lower jaw is as wide as possible, ideal for incoming adult teeth. Never sac-rifice overall balance and har-mony for a fabulous head. Judges will view the whole pic-ture not just the dog's head.

Note the way your choice moves. The Boxer, even in pup-pyhood, should show clean movement with no tendency to stumble or drag the hind feet. Boxers tend to be awkward in their puppy months, so do not confuse this immature lack of coordination with something serious. It's best to take along an experienced Boxer person if you are very concerned about the structure of the puppy. This tends to be a show-dog concern more than a pet concern, though we all want Boxers that can move easily and effortlessly. In evaluating the structure of your pup, consider that the topline (along his back) should be as straight as possible, with the shoulders sloping and the back short. Avoid toplines that 'roach' toward the centre (rise noticeably), weak rear quarters, poor feet, and of course shy or spooky temperaments.

The puppy's bite should be somewhat undershot, meaning the lower jaw protrudes further than the upper jaw. Look for a lower jaw line that is as wide as possible. Be sure that the tongue doesn't stick out when the puppy closes his mouth. The bite is important for show dogs as well as pet dogs. Although your pet puppy won't be disqualified at the dinner table for

DID YOU KNOW?

Two important documents you will get from the breeder are the pup's pedigree and registration papers. The breeder should register the litter and each pup with The Kennel Club, and it is necessary for you to have the paperwork if you plan on showing or breeding in the future.

Make sure you know the breeder's intentions on which type of registration he will obtain for the pup. There are limited registrations which may prohibit the dog from being shown or from competing in non-conformation trials such as Working or Agility if the breeder feels that the pup is not of sufficient quality to do so. There is also a type of registration that will permit the dog in non-conformation competition only.

If your dog is registered with a Kennel-Club-recognised breed club, then you can register the pup with The Kennel Club yourself. Your breeder can assist you with the specifics of the registration process.

an incorrect bite, he may not be able to eat and breathe comfortably throughout his life.

COMMITMENT OF OWNERSHIP

After considering all of these factors, you have most likely already made some very important decisions about selecting your puppy. You have chosen a Boxer, which means that you

Boxer puppies should be playful, lively and fast. They should be out-going and neither shy nor frightened.

When you bring your Boxer puppy home, he should have a crate or bed...someplace to which he can retreat for a nap. If a proper place is not available, he might well just fall asleep in the middle of your dining room.

have decided which characteristics you want in a dog and what type of dog will best fit into your family and lifestyle. If you have selected a breeder, you have gone a step further—you have done your research and found a responsible, conscientious person who breeds quality Boxers and who should be a reliable source of help as you and your puppy adjust to life together. If you have observed a litter in action, you have

DID YOU KNOW?
Unfortunately, when a puppy is purchased by someone who does not take into consideration the time and attention that dog ownership requires, it is the puppy who suffers when he is either abandoned or placed in a shelter by a frustrated owner. So all of the 'homework' you do in preparation for your pup's arrival will benefit you both. The more informed you are, the more you will know what to expect and the better equipped you will be to handle the ups and downs of raising a puppy. Hopefully, everyone in the household is willing to do his part in raising and caring for the pup. The anticipation of owning a dog often brings a lot of promises from excited family members: 'I will walk him every day,' 'I will feed him,' 'I will housebreak him,' etc., but these things take time and effort, and promises can easily be forgotten once the novelty of the new pet has worn off.

obtained a firsthand look at the dynamics of a puppy 'pack' and, thus, you have gotten to learn about each pup's individual personality—perhaps you have even found one that particularly appeals to you.

However, even if you have not yet found the Boxer puppy of your dreams, observing pups will help you learn to recognise certain behaviour and to determine what a pup's behaviour indicates about his temperament. You will be able to pick out which pups are the leaders, which ones are less outgoing, which ones are confident, which ones are shy, playful, friendly, aggressive, etc. Equally as important, you will learn to recognise what a healthy pup should look and act like. All of these things will help you in your search, and when you find the Boxer that was meant for you, you will know it!

Researching your breed, selecting a responsible breeder and observing as many pups as possible are all important steps on the way to dog ownership. It may seem like a lot of effort…and you have not even brought the pup home yet! Remember, though, you cannot be too careful when it comes to deciding on the type of dog you want and finding out about your prospective pup's background. Buying a puppy is not—or should not be—just another whimsical purchase. In fact, this is one instance in which you actually do get to choose your own family! But, you may be thinking, buying a puppy should be fun—it should not be so serious and so much work. If you keep in mind the thought that your puppy is not a cuddly stuffed toy or decorative lawn ornament, but instead will become a real member of your family, you will realise that, while buying a puppy is a plea-surable and exciting endeavour, it is not something to be taken lightly. Relax…the fun will start when the pup comes home!

DID YOU KNOW?
Your breeder may have offered a health guarantee. If not, do not feel awkward about asking for one as part of your sales agreement. An honest and reputable breeder will not be insulted. A health guarantee states that the breeder will take the pup back and give the buyer a refund if the vet dis-covers a problem. A health guarantee may also cover any hereditary diseases that show up before a certain age, in which case the breeder would provide a replacement. The exact terms will differ depending on what is discussed and put in writing between the breeder and the buyer, just make sure that you are in accord with the terms before you agree to purchase the pup and that you read all paperwork carefully.

Always keep in mind that a puppy is nothing more than a baby in a furry disguise…a baby who is virtually helpless in a human world and who trusts his owner for fulfilment of his basic needs for survival. That goes beyond food, water and shelter; your pup needs care, protection, guidance and love. If you are not prepared to commit to this, then you are not pre-pared to own a dog.

Wait a minute, you say. How hard could this be? All of my neighbours own dogs and they seem to be doing just fine. Why should I have to worry about all of this? Well, you should not

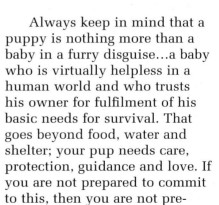

Just yesterday your Boxer pup was playing, sleeping and eat-ing with its sib-lings. The first day in your home is a com-pletely new experience for your new charge.

worry about it; in fact, you will probably find that once your Boxer pup gets used to his new home, he will fall into his place in the family quite naturally. But it never hurts to emphasize the commitment of dog ownership. With some time and patience, it is really not too difficult to raise a curious and exuberant Boxer pup to be a well-adjusted and well-mannered adult dog—a dog that could be your most loyal friend.

PREPARING PUPPY'S PLACE IN YOUR HOME

Researching your breed and finding a breeder are only two aspects of the 'homework' you will have to do before bringing your Boxer puppy home. You will also have to prepare your home and family for the new addition. Much like you would prepare a nursery for a newborn baby, you will need to designate a place in your home that will be the puppy's own. How you prepare your home will depend on how much freedom the dog will be allowed: will he be confined to one room or a specific area in the house, or will he be allowed to roam as he pleases?

It only takes a short time before your Boxer puppy becomes a well-mannered adult who will fit into your lifestyle and make himself comfortable in most family situations.

Will he spend most of his time in the house or will he have an outdoor house too? Whatever you decide, you must ensure that he has a place that he can 'call his own.'

When you bring your new puppy into your home, you are bringing him into what will become his home as well. Obviously, you did not buy a puppy so that he could take over your house, but in order for a puppy to grow into a stable, well-adjusted dog, he has to feel comfortable in his surroundings. Remember, he is leaving the warmth and security of his mother and littermates, plus the familiarity of the only place he has ever known, so it is important to make his transition as easy as possible. By preparing a place in your home for the puppy, you are making him feel as welcome as possible in a strange new place. It should not take him long to get used to it, but the sudden shock of being transplanted is somewhat traumatic for a young pup. Imagine how a small child would feel in the same situation—that is how your puppy must be feeling. It is up to you to reassure him and to let him know, 'Little fellow, you are going to like it here!'

WHAT YOU SHOULD BUY
CRATE
To someone unfamiliar with the use of crates in dog training, it may seem like punishment to shut a dog in a crate; this is not the case at all. Crates are not cruel—crates have many humane and highly effective uses in dog care and training. For example, crate training is a

DID YOU KNOW?
Never line your pup's sleeping area with newspaper. Puppy litters are usually raised on newspaper and, once in your home, the puppy will immediately associate newspaper with voiding. Never put newspaper on any floor while housetraining, as this will only confuse the puppy. If you are paper-training him, use paper in his designated relief area ONLY. Finally, restrict water intake after evening meals. Offer a few licks at a time—never let a young puppy gulp water after meals.

You will have to be prepared for bringing a new puppy home. Keep in mind that your puppy has always been surrounded with other Boxers, other puppies and even other people. You have become the substitute 'pack.' Are you ready for this?

PHOTO COURTESY OF MIKKI PET PRODUCTS.

Like his ancestors, he too will seek out the comfort and retreat of a den—you just happen to be providing him with something a little more luxurious than leaves and twigs lining a dirty ditch.

As far as purchasing a crate, the type that you buy is up to you. It will most likely be one of the two most popular types: wire or fibreglass. There are advantages and disadvantages to each type. For example, a wire crate is more open, allowing the air to flow through and affording the dog a view of what is going on around him. A fibreglass crate, however, is sturdier and can double as a travel crate since it provides more protection for the dog. The size of the

very popular and very successful housebreaking method; a crate can keep your dog safe during travel; and, perhaps most importantly, a crate provides your dog with a place of his own in your home. It serves as a 'doggie bedroom' of sorts—your Boxer can curl up in his crate when he wants to sleep or when he just needs a break. Many dogs sleep in their crates overnight. When lined with soft blankets and filled with his favourite toys, a crate becomes a cosy pseudo-den for your dog.

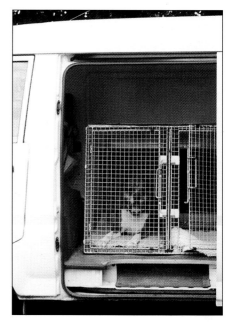

crate is another thing to consider. Puppies do not stay puppies forever—in fact, sometimes it seems as if they grow right before your eyes. A Yorkie-sized crate may be fine for a very young Boxer pup, but it will not do him much good for long! Unless you have the money and the inclination to buy a new crate every time your pup has a growth spurt, it is better to get one that will accommodate your dog both as a pup and at full size. A large crate will be necessary for a full-grown Boxer, as their approximate weight range is between 55 and 70 pounds.

DID YOU KNOW?

During crate training, you should partition off the section of the crate in which the pup stays. If he is given too big of an area, this will hinder your training efforts. Crate training is based on the fact that a dog does not like to soil his sleeping quarters, so it is ineffective to keep a pup in a crate that is so big that he can eliminate in one end and get far enough away from it to sleep. Also, you want to make the crate den-like for the pup. Blankets and toys will make the crate cosy for the small Boxer; as he grows, you may want to evict some of his 'roommates' to make more room.

It will take some coaxing at first, but be patient. Given some time to get used to it, your pup will adapt to his new home-within-a-home quite nicely.

BLANKETS

A blanket or two in the dog's crate will help the dog feel more at home. First, the blankets will take the place of the leaves, twigs, etc., that the pup would use in the wild to make a den; the pup can make his own 'burrow' in the crate. Although your pup is far removed from his den-making ancestors, the denning instinct is still a part of his genetic makeup. Second, until you bring your pup home, he has been sleeping amidst the warmth of his mother and littermates, and while a blanket is not the same as a warm, breath-

Not only are crates valuable for training, but dogs whose ears have been cropped, or who have undergone other surgical procedures, can be securely isolated for recuperation.

Pet shops offer a multitude of safe dog toys. Only buy your dog toys from a pet shop, as many toys are unsuitable for dogs because they may be easily torn. If small pieces of vinyl toys are swallowed, they may cause a blockage that will require surgical intervention.

ing body, it still provides heat and something with which to snuggle. You will want to wash your pup's blankets frequently in case he has an accident in his crate, and replace or remove any blanket that becomes ragged and starts to fall apart.

TOYS

Toys are a must for dogs of all ages, especially for curious playful pups. Puppies are the 'children' of the dog world, and what child does not love toys? Chew toys provide enjoyment to both dog and owner—your dog will enjoy playing with his favourite toys, while you will enjoy the fact that they distract him from your expensive shoes and leather sofa. Puppies love to chew; in

You can tell who is the dominant dog in this group! A dog bed is a must for your puppy. Pet shops have many styles in different shapes, sizes and types of material. Get one BEFORE you bring the puppy home.

fact, chewing is a physical need for pups as they are teething, and everything looks appetising! The full range of your possessions—from old dishrag to Oriental rug—are fair game in the eyes of a teething pup. Puppies are not all that discerning when it comes to finding something to literally 'sink their teeth into'—everything tastes great!

Stuffed toys are another option; these are good to put in the dog's crate to give him some company. Be careful of these, as a pup can de-stuff one pretty quick-

Be careful of natural bones, which have a tendency to splinter into sharp, dangerous pieces. Also be careful of rawhide, which after enough chewing can turn into pieces that are easy to swallow, and also watch out for the mushy mess it can turn into on your carpet.

DID YOU KNOW?

Chewing goes hand in hand with nipping in the sense that a teething puppy is always looking for a way to soothe his aching gums. In this case, instead of chewing on you, he may have taken a liking to your favourite shoe or something else which he should not be chewing. Again, realise that this is a normal canine behaviour that does not need to be discouraged, only redirected. Your pup just needs to be taught what is acceptable to chew on and what is off limits. Consistently tell him NO when you catch him chewing on something forbidden and give him a chew toy. Conversely, praise him when you catch him chewing on something appropriate. In this way you are discouraging the inappropriate behaviour and reinforcing the desired behaviour. The puppy chewing should stop after his adult teeth have come in, but most adult dogs continue to chew for various reasons—perhaps because he is bored, perhaps to relieve tension, or perhaps he just likes to chew. That is why it is important to redirect his chewing when he is still young.

ly, and stay away from stuffed toys with small plastic eyes or parts that a pup could choke on. Similarly, squeaky toys are quite popular. There are dogs that will come running from anywhere in the house at the first sound from their favourite squeaky friend. Again, if a pup de-stuffs one of these, the small plastic squeaker inside can be dangerous if swallowed. Monitor the condition of your pup's toys carefully and get rid of any that have been chewed to the point of becoming potentially dangerous.

walking and safety purposes, the nylon lead is a good choice. As your pup grows up and gets used to walking on the lead, and can do it politely, you may want to purchase a flexible lead, which allows you either to extend the length to give the dog a broader area to explore or to pull in the lead when you want to keep him close. Of course there are special leads for training purposes, and specially made leather harnesses for the working Boxer, but these are not necessary for routine walks. If your Boxer is especially strong or tends to pull on the lead, you may want to purchase something stronger, like a thicker leather lead.

Pet shops usually carry an extensive range of leads. A nylon lead is probably the best option as your Boxer puppy's first lead.

LEAD

A nylon lead is probably the best option as it is the most resistant to puppy teeth should your pup take a liking to chewing on his lead. Of course, this is a habit that should be nipped in the bud, but if your pup likes to chew on his lead he has a very slim chance of being able to chew through the strong nylon. Nylon leads are also lightweight, which is good for a young Boxer who is just getting used to the idea of walking on a lead. For everyday

COLLAR

Your pup should get used to wearing a collar all the time since you will want to attach his ID tags to his collar. Also, the lead and collar go hand in hand—you have to attach the lead to something! A light-weight nylon collar will be a good choice; make sure that it fits snugly enough so that the pup cannot wriggle out of it, but loose enough so that it will not be uncomfortably tight around the pup's neck. You should be able to fit a finger in between the pup and the collar. It may take some time for your pup to get used to wearing the collar,

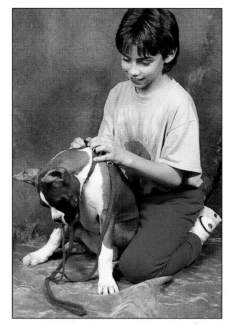

Your Boxer puppy should be introduced to the collar and lead as soon as possible. It may take a few days for your puppy to become accustomed to a collar. Start with a lightweight nylon collar that is snug enough so the puppy cannot wriggle out of it.

You will need bowls for food and water. Most breeders opt for stainless steel bowls since they are the most convenient. They can be sanitised, and the pups cannot chew them.

Your local pet shop will be able to show you a wide range of food and water bowls. Select the size, colour and price range which best suits you and your Boxer.

but soon he will not even notice that it is there. Choke collars are made for training, but should only be used by an owner who knows exactly how to use it. If you use a stronger leather lead or a chain lead to walk your Boxer, you will need a stronger collar as well.

FOOD AND WATER BOWLS

Your pup will need two bowls, one for food and one for water. You may want two sets of bowls, one for inside and one for outside, depending on where the dog will be fed and where he will be spending most of his time. Stainless steel or sturdy plastic bowls are popular choices. Although plastic bowls are more chewable, dogs tend not to chew on the steel variety, which can also be sterilised. Some dog owners like to put their dogs' food and water bowls on a specially made elevated stand; this brings the food closer to the dog's level so he does not have to bend down as far, thus aiding his digestion and helping to guard against bloat or gastric torsion in deep-chested dogs. The most important thing is to buy sturdy bowls since, again, anything is in danger of being chewed by puppy teeth and you do not want your dog to be constantly chewing apart his bowl (for his safety and for your wallet!).

CLEANING SUPPLIES
A pup that is not housetrained means you will be doing a lot of cleaning until he is. Accidents will occur, which is okay for now because he does not know any better. All you can do is clean up any 'accidents'—old rags, towels, newspapers and a safe disinfectant are good to have on hand.

BEYOND THE BASICS
The items previously discussed are the bare necessities. You will find out what else you need as you go along—grooming supplies, flea/tick protection, baby gates to partition a room, etc.—these things will vary depending on your situation. It is just important that right away you have everything

you need to feed and make your Boxer comfortable in his first few days at home.

PUPPY-PROOFING YOUR HOME
Aside from making sure that your Boxer will be comfortable in your home, you also have to make sure that your home is safe for your Boxer. This means taking precautions to make sure that your pup will not get into anything he should not get into and that there is nothing within his reach that may harm him should he sniff it, chew it, inspect it, etc. This probably seems obvious since, while you are primarily concerned with your pup's safety, at the same time you do not want your belongings to be ruined. Breakables should be placed out of reach if your dog is to have

You will need something to assist you in cleaning up after your Boxer has relieved himself. Pet shops usually have several gadgets suitable for sanitary collection and disposal of waste.

DID YOU KNOW?
By providing sleeping and resting quarters that fit the dog, and offering frequent opportunities to relieve himself outside his quarters, the puppy quickly learns that the outdoors (or the newspaper if you are training him to paper) is the place to go when he needs to urinate or defecate. It also reinforces his innate desire to keep his sleeping quarters clean. This, in turn, helps develop the muscle control that will eventually produce a dog with clean living habits.

full run of the house. If he is to be limited to certain places within the house, keep any potentially dangerous items in the 'off-limits' areas. An electrical cord can pose a danger should the puppy decide to taste it—and who is going to convince a pup that it would not make a great chew toy? Cords should be or fastened tightly against the wall. If your dog is going to spend time in a crate, make sure that there is nothing near his crate that he can reach if he sticks his curious little nose or paws through the openings. And just as you would with a child, keep all household cleaners and chemicals where the pup cannot get to them.

It is just as important to make sure that the outside of your home is safe. Of course your puppy should never be unsupervised, but a pup let loose in the garden will want to run and explore, and he should be granted that freedom. Do not let a fence give you a false sense of security; you would be surprised how crafty (and persistent) a dog can be in figuring out how to dig under and squeeze his way through small holes, or to jump or climb over a fence. The remedy is to make the fence high enough so that it really is impossible for your dog to get over it (about 3 metres should suffice), and well embedded into the ground. Be sure to repair or secure any gaps in the fence. Check the fence periodically to ensure that it is in good shape and make repairs as need-

You can safely take your Boxer puppy along on a picnic. Just bring his crate in case he gets too frisky.

Boxers have very individual personalities. This fellow likes to collect sticks. Take advantage of these natural instincts and train the dog to bring you the newspapers or your slippers.

ed; a very determined pup may return to the same spot to 'work on it' until he is able to get through.

FIRST TRIP TO THE VET

Okay, you have picked out your puppy, your home and family are ready, now all you have to do is pick your Boxer up from the breeder and the fun begins, right? Well...not so fast. Something else you need to prepare for is your pup's first trip to the veterinary surgeon. Perhaps the breeder can recommend someone in the area that specialises in Boxers, or maybe you know some other Boxer owners who can suggest a good vet. Either way, you should have an appointment arranged for your pup before you pick

him up; plan on taking him for a checkup within the first few days of bringing him home.

The pup's first visit will consist of an overall examination to make sure that the pup does not have any problems that

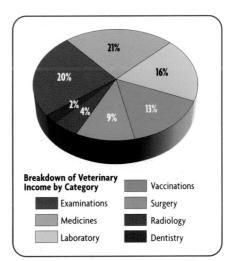

Breakdown of Veterinary Income by Category

- Examinations
- Medicines
- Laboratory
- Vaccinations
- Surgery
- Radiology
- Dentistry

21%
16%
20%
2%
4%
9%
13%

Veterinary surgeons are extremely skilful. They must be completely educated in medicine, surgery, anaesthetics, dentistry, radiology and laboratory techniques. The chart indicates the average percentage of income that vets earn for their services.

59

are not apparent to the eye. The veterinary surgeon will also set up a schedule for the pup's vaccinations; the breeder will inform you of which ones the pup has already received and the vet can continue from there.

INTRODUCTION TO THE FAMILY

Everyone in the house will be excited about the puppy coming home and will want to pet him and play with him, but it is best to make the introduction low-key so as not to overwhelm the puppy. He is apprehensive already; it is the first time he has been separated from his mother and the breeder, and the ride to your home is likely the first time he has been in an auto. The last thing you want to do is smother him, as this will only frighten him further. This is not to say that human contact is not extremely necessary at this stage, because this is the time when an instant connection between the pup and his human family are formed. Gentle petting and soothing words should help console him, as well as just putting him down and letting him explore on his own (under your watchful eye, of course).

The pup may approach the family members or may busy himself with exploring for awhile. Gradually, each person should spend some time with the pup, one at a time, crouching down to get as close to the pup's level as possible and letting him sniff their hands and petting him gently. He definitely needs human attention and he needs to be touched—this is how to form an immediate bond. Just remember that the pup is experiencing a lot of things for the first time, all at the same time. There are new people, new noises, new smells, and new things to investigate; so be gentle, be affectionate and be as comforting as you can be.

DID YOU KNOW?

The majority of problems that are commonly seen in young pups will disappear as your Boxer gets older. However, how you deal with problems when he is young will determine how he reacts to discipline as an adult dog. It is important to establish who is boss (hopefully it will be you!) right away when you are first bonding with your Boxer. This bond will set the tone for the rest of your life together.

YOUR PUP'S FIRST NIGHT HOME

You have travelled home with your new charge safely in his basket or crate. He's been to the vet for a thorough check-over; he's been weighed, his papers examined; perhaps he's even been vaccinated and wormed as well. He's met the family, licked the whole family, including the excited children and the less-than-happy cat. He's explored his area, his new bed, the garden and anywhere else he's been permitted. He's eaten his first meal at home and relieved himself in the proper place. He's heard lots of new sounds, smelled new friends and seen more of the outside world than ever before.

That was just the first day! He's tuckered out and is ready for bed…or so you think!

It's puppy's first night and you are ready to say 'Good

night'—keep in mind that this is puppy's first night ever to be sleeping alone. His dam and littermates are no longer at paw's length and he's a bit scared, cold and lonely. Be reassuring to your new family member. This is not the time to spoil him and give in to his inevitable whining.

Puppies whine. They whine to let the others know where they are and hopefully to get company out of it. Place your pup in his new bed or crate in his room and close the door. Mercifully, he will fall asleep without a peep. If the inevitable occurs, ignore the whining; he is fine. Be strong and keep his interest in mind. Do not allow your heart to become guilty and visit the pup. He will fall asleep.

Many breeders recommend placing a piece of bedding from his former homestead in his new bed so that he recognises the scent of his littermates. Others still advise placing a hot water bottle in his bed for warmth. This latter may be a

Never allow your dog to be unrestrained in your car or caravan. The dog could be hurt if you stop abruptly, or you can be distracted if the dog jumps onto your lap whilst you are concentrating on driving.

61

Keep your eye on your Boxer puppy when he is released in the garden. A koi pond is lovely, but it can be dangerous if a puppy decides to chase a fish!

good idea provided the pup doesn't attempt to suckle—he'll get good and wet and may not fall asleep so fast.

Puppy's first night can be somewhat stressful for the pup and his new family. Remember that you are setting the tone of nighttime at your house. Unless you want to play with your pup every evening at 10 p.m., midnight and 2 a.m., don't initiate the habit. Surely your family will thank you, and so will your pup!

PREVENTING PUPPY PROBLEMS
SOCIALISATION
Now that you have done all of the preparatory work and have helped your pup get accustomed to his new home and family, it is about time for you to have some fun! Socialising your Boxer pup gives you the

opportunity to show off your new friend, and your pup gets to reap the benefits of being an adorable furry creature that people will coo over, want to pet and, in general, think is absolutely precious!

Besides getting to know his new family, your puppy should be exposed to other people, animals and situations. This will help him become well adjusted as he grows up and less prone to being timid or fearful of the new things he will encounter. Your pup's socialisation began at the breeder's, now it is your

There is no better entertainment for a Boxer puppy of any age than to play with his human friends.

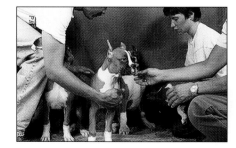

responsibility to continue. The socialisation he receives up until the age of 12 weeks is the most critical, as this is the time when he forms his impressions of the outside world. Lack of socialisation can manifest itself in fear and aggression as the dog grows up. He needs lots of human contact, affection, handling and exposure to other animals. Be careful during the eight-to-ten-week period, also known as the fear period. The interaction he receives during this time should be gentle and reassuring.

Once your pup has received his necessary vaccinations, feel free to take him out and about (on his lead, of course). Take him around the neighbourhood, take him on your daily errands, let people pet him, let him meet

DID YOU KNOW?

Thorough socialisation includes not only meeting new people but also being introduced to new experiences such as riding in the auto, having his coat brushed, hearing the television, walking in a crowd—the list is endless. The more your pup experiences, and the more positive the experiences are, the less of a shock and the less scary it will be for your pup to encounter new things.

other dogs and pets, etc. Puppies do not have to try to make friends; there will be no shortage of people who will want to introduce themselves. Just make sure that you carefully supervise each meeting. If the neighbourhood children want to say hello, for example, that is great—children and pups most often make great companions. But sometimes an excited child can unintentionally handle a pup too roughly, or an overzealous pup can playfully nip a little too hard. You want to make socialisation experiences positive ones; what a pup learns during this very formative stage will impact his attitude toward future encounters. A pup that has a bad experience with a child may grow up to be a dog that is shy around or aggressive toward children, and you want your dog to be comfortable around everyone.

Children's toys are usually unsuitable for Boxer puppies because they are easily shredded, may contain toxic dyes or stuffing or may have wire frames that could injure the dog.

'Just getting to know you!' Puppies and kittens take a little while to become comfortable with one another.

CONSISTENCY IN TRAINING

Dogs, being pack animals, naturally need a leader, or else they try to establish dominance in their packs. When you bring a dog into your family, who becomes the leader and who becomes the 'pack' are entirely up to you! Your pup's intuitive quest for dominance, coupled with the fact that it is nearly impossible to look at an adorable Boxer pup, with his 'puppy-dog' eyes and his too-big-for-his-head-still-floppy ears, and not cave in, give the pup almost an unfair advantage in getting the upper hand! And a pup will definitely test the waters to see what he can and cannot get away with. Do not give in to those pleading eyes—stand your ground when it comes to disciplining the pup and make sure that all family members do the same. It will only confuse the pup when Mother tells him to get off the couch when he is used to sitting up

There is no better way for children and puppies to get acquainted than to meet and to exchange smiles and embraces

there with Father to watch the nightly news. Avoid discrepancies by having all members of the household decide on the rules before the pup even comes home...and be consistent in enforcing them! Early training shapes the dog's personality, so you cannot be unclear in what you expect.

COMMON PUPPY PROBLEMS

The best way to prevent problems is to be proactive in stopping an undesirable behaviour as soon as it starts. The old saying 'You can't teach an old dog new tricks' does not necessarily hold true, but it is true that it is much easier to discourage bad behaviour in a young developing pup than to wait until the pup's bad behaviour becomes the adult dog's bad habit. There are some problems that are especially prevalent in puppies as they develop.

Boxer puppies may look well posed amongst flowering plants, but take care. Many plants are poisonous to dogs.

NIPPING

As puppies start to teethe, they feel the need to sink their teeth into anything...unfortunately that includes your fingers, arms, hair, toes...whatever happens to be available. You may find this behaviour cute for about the first five seconds ...until you feel just how sharp those puppy teeth are. This is something you want to discourage immediately and consistently with a firm 'No!' (or whatever number of firm 'No's' it takes for him to understand that you mean business) and replace your finger with an appropriate chew toy. While this behaviour is merely annoying when the dog is still young, it can become dangerous as your Boxer's adult teeth grow in and his jaws develop, if he thinks that it is okay to gnaw on human appendages. You do not want to take a chance with a Boxer, this is a breed whose jaws become naturally very strong. He does not mean any harm with a friendly nip, but he also does not know his own strength.

CRYING/WHINING

Your pup will often cry, whine, whimper, howl or make some type of commotion when he is left alone. This is basically his way of calling out for attention, of calling out to make sure that you know he is there and that you have not forgotten about him. He feels insecure when he is left alone, for example, when you are out of the house and he is in his crate or when you are in another part of the house and he cannot see you. The noise he is making is an expression of the anxiety he feels at being alone, so he needs to be taught that being alone is okay. You are not actually training the dog to stop making noise, you are training him to feel comfortable when he is alone and thus

DID YOU KNOW?

Young dogs with a timid personality and temperament are much easier to train than more assertive dogs. If you have a puppy that seems untrainable, take him to a trainer or behaviourist. The dog may have a personality problem that requires the help of a professional, or perhaps you need help in learning how to train your dog.

removing the need for him to make the noise. This is where the crate filled with cosy blankets and toys comes in handy. You want to know that he is safe when you are not there to supervise, and you know that he will be safe in his crate rather than roaming freely about the house. In order for the pup to stay in his crate without making a fuss, he needs to be comfortable in his crate. On that note, it is extremely important that the crate is never used as a form of punishment, or the pup will have a negative association with the crate.

Accustom the pup to the crate in short, gradually increasing time intervals in which you put him in the crate, maybe with a treat, and stay in the

room with him. If he cries or makes a fuss, do not go to him, but stay in his sight. Gradually he will realise that staying in his crate is all right without your help, and it will not be so traumatic for him when you are not around. You may want to leave the radio on softly when you leave the house; the sound of human voices may be comforting to him.

DID YOU KNOW?

Use treats to bribe your dog into a desired behaviour. Try small pieces of hard cheese or freeze-dried liver. Never offer chocolate as it has toxic qualities for dogs.

The Boxer puppy's face clearly reveals its dependence and needs. A puppy should never have to wonder if his owner loves him.

If the puppy cries or whines when left alone, he is merely communicating his loneliness the only way he knows how.

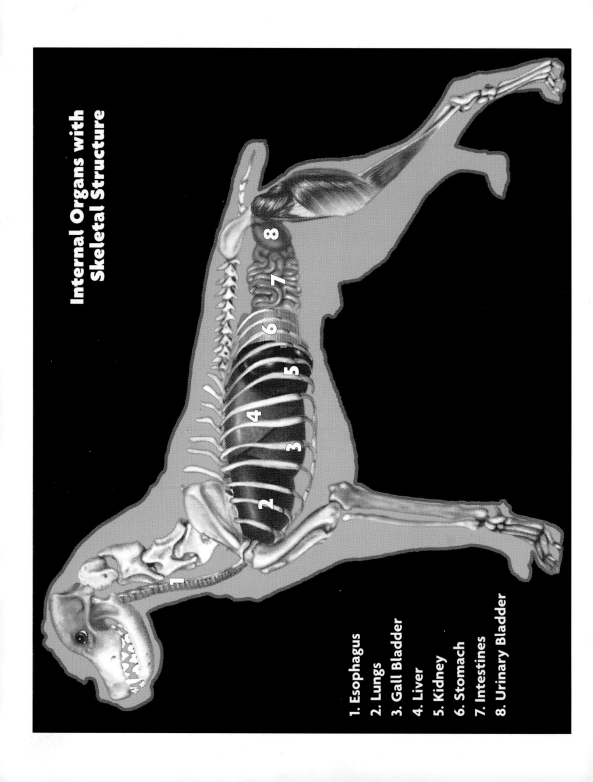

Internal Organs with Skeletal Structure

1. Esophagus
2. Lungs
3. Gall Bladder
4. Liver
5. Kidney
6. Stomach
7. Intestines
8. Urinary Bladder

Everyday Care of Your Boxer

DIETARY AND FEEDING CONSIDERATIONS

In today's world, your Boxer has hundreds of choices for eating. The market offers dozens of brands in dozens of varieties: from the puppy diet lamb and rice to the senior diet to the hypoallergenic to the low-calorie! Since your Boxer's nutrition is related to his coat and health and temperament, you want to offer him the best possible diet, fit for a Boxer his age. Dedicated owners, however, can become very perplexed by the vast number of choices. Even those people who truly want to feed their dogs the best often cannot do so because they do not know which foods are best for their dogs.

Dog foods are produced in three basic types: dry, semi-moist and canned or tinned. Dry foods are for the cost conscious because they are much less expensive than semi-moist and canned. Dry foods contain the least fat and the most preservatives. Most tinned foods are 60–70-percent water, while semi-moist foods are so full of sugar that they are the least preferred by owners, though dogs welcome them (as does a child sweets).

Three stages of development must be considered when selecting a diet for your dog: the puppy stage, the mid-age or adult stage and the senior age or geriatric stage.

PUPPY STAGE

Puppies have a natural instinct to suck milk from their mother's breasts. They should exhibit this behaviour the first day of their lives. If they don't suckle within

Elevated bowl stands are excellent choices for Boxer adults—and they keep the toddlers away from mom's dish.

69

These Boxer puppies need a large area in which to sleep. They probably should be introduced to solid foods, too.

a few hours you should attempt to put them onto their mother's nipple. Their failure to feed means you have to feed them yourself under the advice and guidance of a veterinary surgeon. This will involve a baby bottle and a special formula. Their mother's milk is much better than any formula because it contains colostrum, a sort of antibiotic milk which protects the puppy

Puppies should be weaned when they are six weeks of age.

during the first eight to ten weeks of their lives.

Puppies should be allowed to nurse for six weeks and they should be slowly weaned away from their mother by introducing small portions of tinned meat after they are about one month old.

A mother's milk is much better than any formula because it contains natural antibodies that protect dogs in puppyhood.

By the time they are eight weeks old, they should be completely weaned and fed solely a puppy dry food. During this weaning period, their diet is most important as the puppy grows fastest during its first year of life. Growth foods can be recommended by your veterinary surgeon and the puppy should be kept on this diet for up to 18 months.

Puppy diets should be balanced for your dog's needs and supplements of vitamins, minerals and protein should not be necessary.

Adult Diets
A dog is considered an adult when it has stopped growing. The growth is in height and/or length. Do not consider the dog's weight when the decision is made to switch from a puppy diet to a maintenance diet. Again you should rely upon your veterinary surgeon to recommend an acceptable maintenance diet. Major dog food manufacturers specialise in this type of food and it is just necessary for you to

select the one best suited to your dog's needs. Active dogs may have different requirements than sedate dogs.

A Boxer reaches adulthood at about two years of age, though some dogs fully mature at 16 months, while others may take up to three years.

DIETS FOR SENIOR DOGS

As dogs get older, their metabolism changes. The older dog usually exercises less, moves more slowly and sleeps more. This change in lifestyle and physiological performance requires a change in diet. Since these changes take place slowly, they might not be recognisable. What is easily recognisable is weight gain. By continually feeding your dog an adult

As your the Boxer matures, his diet should be changed. Consult your veterinary surgeon for advice about when to change the diet and the food you should offer.

maintenance diet when it is slowing down metabolically, your dog will gain weight. Obesity in an older dog compounds the health problems that already accompany old age.

As your dog gets older, few of their organs function up to par. The kidneys slow down and the intestines become less efficient. These age-related factors are best handled with a change in diet and a change in feeding schedule to give smaller portions that are more easily digested.

There is no single best diet for every older dog. While many dogs do well on light or senior diets, other dogs do better on puppy diets or other special premium diets such as lamb and rice.

DID YOU KNOW?

Many adult diets are based on grain. There is nothing wrong with this as long as it does not contain soy meal. Diets based on soy often cause flatulence (passing gas).

Grain-based diets are almost always the least expensive and a good grain diet is just as good as the most expensive diet containing animal protein.

There are many cases, however, when your dog might require a special diet. These special requirements should only be recommended by your veterinary surgeon.

What are you feeding your dog?

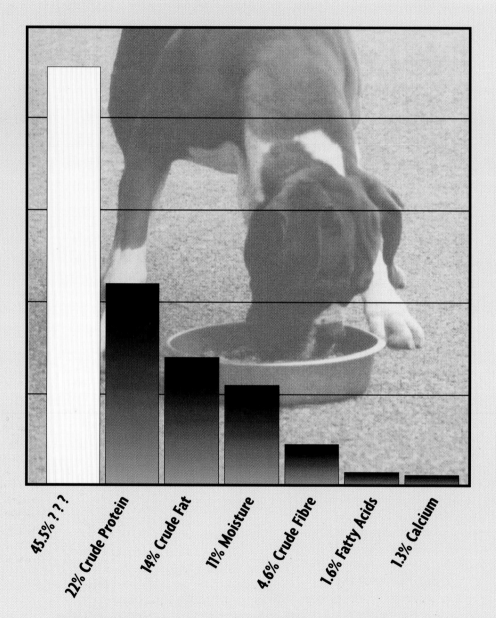

45.5% ? ? ?

22% Crude Protein

14% Crude Fat

11% Moisture

4.6% Crude Fibre

1.6% Fatty Acids

1.3% Calcium

Read the label on your dog food. Most manufacturers merely advise you of 50-55% of the contents, leaving the other 45% in doubt.

Be sensitive to your senior Boxer's diet and this will help control other problems that may arise with your old friend.

WATER

Just as your dog needs proper nutrition from his food, water is an essential "nutrient" as well. Water keeps the dog's body properly hydrated and promotes normal function of the body's systems. During housebreaking it is necessary to keep an eye on how much water your Boxer is drinking, but once he is reliably trained he should have access to clean fresh water at all times. Make sure that the dog's water bowl is clean, and

Placing your hand in the puppy's bowl reinforces trust and reminds the puppy who's the boss. Be sure that your pup has clean water every day and that the bowl is sanitised regularly.

change the water often. As some vets have recommended, do not leave water bowls down when feeding your dog. This practice can help to promote the onset of bloat in the Boxer.

EXERCISE

Exercising a Boxer is not as daunting as it may seem. The Boxer is a working dog, not field dog that has pent-up energy or a track dog that has long legs to stretch. All dogs require some form of exercise, regardless of breed. A sedentary lifestyle is as harmful to a dog as it is to a person. The Boxer happens to be a fairly active breed that requires more exercise than, say, an English Bulldog, but you don't have to be a weightlifter or marathon runner to provide your dog with the exercise he needs. Regular walks, play sessions in the garden, or letting the dog run free in the garden under your supervision are all sufficient forms of exercise for the Boxer. For those who are more

Read the label on your dog food and learn what makes one food better than another. Never assume that the cheapest food is the worst and the most expensive food is the best.

The diet you feed a very active dog should be different than the diet offered to a Boxer kept in the house most of the day. It's always best to encourage exercise!

Most Boxers are very attached to their masters. Unless your Boxer is brushed every few days to remove dead hairs, he will leave a trail on your furniture, carpet and clothes. Regular grooming is also a bonding experience between you and your Boxer.

ambitious, you will find that your Boxer will be able to keep up with you on extra long walks or the morning run. Not only is exercise essential to keep the dog's body fit, it is essential to his mental well-being. A bored dog will find something to do, which often manifests itself in some type of destructive behaviour. In this sense, it is essential for the owner's mental well-being as well!

Most Boxers enjoy being brushed. If possible, brush your dog outdoors so the dead hairs, dandruff, dried skin and debris can more readily be disposed of.

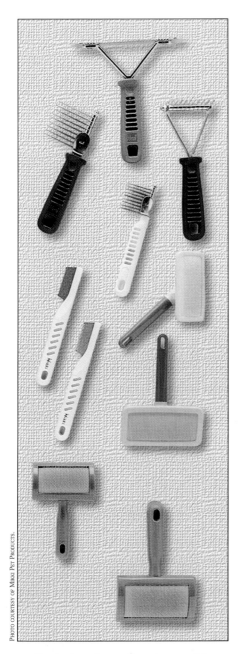

PHOTO COURTESY OF MIKKI PET PRODUCTS.

Your local pet shop usually carries a complete range of grooming tools at reasonable prices.

GROOMING

BRUSHING

A natural bristle brush, a slicker brush, or even a hound glove can be used for regular routine brushing. Grooming is effective for removing dead hair and stimulating the dog's natural oils to add shine and a healthy look to the coat. Your Boxer is not a breed that needs excessive grooming, but his coat needs to be brushed every few days as part of routine maintenance. Regular brushing will get rid of dust and dandruff and remove any dead hair. Regular grooming sessions are also a good way to spend time with your dog. Many dogs

Brushes should be cleaned in between uses to remove possible contamination with parasites or their eggs and larvae.

Most Boxers enjoy water and being bathed. When the temperature permits, you can bathe your Boxer outdoors. If using a water hose for rinsing, do not direct the stream of water at the dog's face, ears or genital area.

grow to like the feel of being brushed and will enjoy the daily routine.

BATHING

Dogs do not need to be bathed as often as humans, but regular

bathing is essential for healthy skin and a healthy, shiny coat. Again, like most anything, if you accustom your pup to being bathed as a puppy, it will be second nature by the time he grows up. You want your dog to

be at ease in the bath or else it could end up a wet, soapy, messy ordeal for both of you!

Brush your Boxer thoroughly before wetting his coat. This will get rid of most of the dead coat. Make that your dog has a good non-slip surface to stand on. Begin by wetting the dog's coat. A shower or hose attachment is necessary for thoroughly wetting and rinsing the coat. Check the water temperature to make sure that it is neither too hot nor too cold.

Next, apply shampoo to the dog's coat and work it into a good lather. You should purchase a shampoo that is made for dogs; do not use a product made for human hair. Washing the head last; you do not want shampoo to drip into the dog's eyes while you are washing the rest of his body. Work the shampoo all the way down to the skin. You can use this opportunity to check the skin for any bumps, bites or other abnormalities. Do not neglect any area of the body—get all of the hard-to-reach places.

Once the dog has been thoroughly shampooed, he requires an equally thorough rinsing. Shampoo left in the coat can be irritating to the skin. Protect his eyes from the shampoo by shielding them with your hand and directing the flow of water in the opposite direction. You should

Clean your Boxer's ears regularly. Be on the alert for any sign of infection, inflammation or ear mite infestation. Unless you are skilled, do NOT probe the ear with anything rigid.

also avoid getting water in the ear canal. Be prepared for your dog to shake out his coat—you

DID YOU KNOW?

How much grooming equipment you purchase will depend on how much grooming you are going to do. Here are some basics for the Boxer:

- Natural bristle brush
- Slicker brush
- Scissors
- Blaster
- Electric clippers
- Rubber mat
- Dog shampoo
- Spray hose attachment
- Ear cleaner
- Cotton buds
- Heavy towels
- Nail clippers

Cotton buds, disposable after use, are recommended for the healthy maintenance of your Boxer's ears.

might want to stand back, but make sure you have a hold on the dog to keep him from running through the house.

EAR CLEANING
The ears should be kept clean and any excess hair inside the ear should be trimmed. Ears can be cleaned with a cotton bud and special cleaner or ear powder made especially for dogs. Be on the lookout for any signs of infection or ear mite infestation. If your Boxer has been shaking his head or scratching at his ears frequently, this usually indicates a problem. If his ears have an unusual odour, this is a sure sign of mite infestation or infection, and a signal to have his ears checked by the veterinary surgeon.

NAIL CLIPPING
Your Boxer should be accustomed to having his nails trimmed at an early age, since it will be part of your maintenance routine throughout his life. Not only does it look nicer, but a dog with long nails can cause injury if he jumps up or if he scratches someone unintentionally. Also, a long nail has a better chance of ripping and bleeding, or causing the feet to spread. A good rule of thumb is that if you can hear your dog's nails clicking on the floor when he walks, his nails are too long.

Before you start cutting, make sure you can identify the 'quick' in each nail. The quick is a blood

DID YOU KNOW?
A dog that spends a lot of time outside on a hard surface such as cement or pavement will have his nails naturally worn down and may not need to have them trimmed as often, except maybe in the colder months when he is not outside as much. Regardless, it is best to get your Boxer accustomed to this procedure at an early age so that he is used to it. Some dogs are especially sensitive about having their feet touched, but if a dog has experienced it since he was young, he should not be bothered by it.

Your Boxer's nails will require clipping throughout his life. You should learn how to clip your Boxer's nails and accustom your dog to the routine while he is still a puppy.

vessel that runs through the centre of each nail and grows rather close to the end. It will bleed if accidentally cut, which will be quite painful for the dog as it contains nerve endings. Keep some type of clotting agent on hand, such as a styptic pencil or styptic powder (the type used for shaving). This will stop the bleeding quickly when applied to the end of the cut nail. Do not panic if this happens, just stop the bleeding and talk soothingly to your dog. Once he has calmed down, move on to the next nail. It is better to clip a little at a time, particularly with black-nailed dogs.

Immaculate grooming requires trimming excess hair growth wherever it occurs.

Caring for your Boxer's teeth requires regular brushing and use of dental chewing devices available from your pet shop. Use special toothbrushes designed specifically for dogs.

79

There are scissors with rounded tips to trim facial hairs and whiskers from your Boxer's face, if so desired.

Hold your pup steady as you begin trimming his nails; you do not want him to make any sudden movements or run away. Talk to him soothingly and stroke his fur as you clip. Holding his foot in your hand, simply take off the end of each nail in one quick clip. You can purchase nail clippers that are specially made for dogs; you can probably find them wherever you buy pet or grooming supplies.

TRAVELLING WITH YOUR DOG
AUTOMOBILE TRAVEL
You should accustom your Boxer

There are special crates in which your Boxer can be safely transported in your vehicle. Never allow the dog unrestrained freedom while you are driving.

to riding in an car at an early age. You may or may not often take him in the car, but at the very least he will need to go to the vet and you do not want these trips to be traumatic for the dog or a big hassle for you. The safest way for a dog to ride in the car is in his crate. If he uses a fibreglass crate in the house, you can use the same crate for travel. If you have a wire crate in the house, consider

---

DID YOU KNOW?

A point that deserves mentioning is never leave your dog alone in the auto. In hot weather your dog can die from the high temperature inside a closed vehicle, and leaving the window open is dangerous as well since the dog can hurt himself trying to get out.

---

purchasing an appropriately sized fibreglass or wooden crate for travelling. Wire crates can be used for travel, but fibreglass or wooden crates are safer.

Put the pup in the crate and see how he reacts. If he seems uneasy, you can have a passenger hold him on his lap while you drive. Another option is a specially made safety harness for dogs, which straps the dog in much like a seat belt. Do not let the dog roam loose in the vehicle—this is very dangerous! If you should stop short, your

ments. It is rather common for dogs to travel by air, but advance permission is usually required. The dog will be required to travel in a fibreglass crate; you may be able to use your own or the airline can usually supply one. To help the dog be at ease, put one of his favourite toys in the crate with him. Do not feed the dog for at least six hours before the trip to minimise his need to relieve himself. However, certain regulations specify that water must always be made available to the dog in the crate.

Make sure your dog is properly identified and that your contact information appears on

Special restraining halters can be used on many occasions. Your car can be outfitted with a strong lead to be attached to a halter for use when transporting your Boxer. Other options include your car safety belt.

dog can be thrown and injured. If the dog starts climbing on you and pestering you while you are driving, you will not be able to concentrate on the road. It is an unsafe situation for everyone—human and canine.

For long trips, be prepared to stop to let the dog relieve himself. Bring along whatever you need to clean up after him. You should bring along some old towels and rags, should he have an accident in the car or become carsick.

AIR TRAVEL
If bringing your dog on a flight, you will have to contact the airline to make special arrange-

> **DID YOU KNOW?**
> For international travel you will have to make arrangements well in advance (perhaps months), as countries' regulations pertaining to bringing in animals differ. There may be special health certificates and/or vaccinations that your dog will need before taking the trip, sometimes this has to be done within a certain time frame. In rabies-free countries, you will need to bring proof of the dog's rabies vaccination and there may be a quarantine period upon arrival.

his ID tags and on his crate. Animals travel in a different area of the plane than human passengers, and, although transporting animals is routine for large airlines, there is always that slight risk of getting separated from your dog.

BOARDING

So you want to take a family holiday—and you want to include all members of the family. You would probably make arrangements for accommodations ahead of time anyway, but this is especially important when travelling with a dog. You do not want to make an overnight stop at the only place around for miles to find out that they do not allow dogs. Also, you do not want to reserve a place for your family without mentioning that you are bringing a dog, because if it is against their policy you may not have a place to stay.

Alternatively, if you are travelling and choose not to bring

Bonding is required between dogs as well as between people. Unless dogs know each other, they should be supervised, especially when one is much smaller than the other.

your Boxer, you will have to make arrangements for him while you are away. Some options are to bring him to a neighbour's house to stay while you are gone, to have a trusted neighbour stop by often or stay at your house, or bring your dog to a reputable boarding kennel. If you choose to board him at a kennel, you should stop by to see the facility and where the dogs are kept to make sure that it is clean. Talk to some of the employees and see how they treat the dogs—do they spend time with the dogs, play with them, exercise them, etc.? You know that your Boxer will not be happy unless he gets regular activity. Also find out the kennel's policy on vaccinations and what they require. This is for all of the dogs' safety, since when dogs are kept together, there is a greater risk of diseases being passed from dog to dog. Many veterinary surgeons offer boarding facilities; this is another option.

IDENTIFICATION

Your Boxer is your valued companion and friend. That is why you always keep a close eye on him and you have made sure that he cannot escape from the garden or wriggle out of his collar and run away from you. However, accidents can happen and there may come a time when your dog unexpectedly gets

DID YOU KNOW?

If your dog gets lost, he is not able to ask for directions home.

Identification tags fastened to the collar give important information—the dog's name, the owner's name, the owner's address and a telephone number where the owner can be reached. This makes it easy for whoever finds the dog to contact the owner and arrange to have the dog returned. An added advantage is that a person will be more likely to approach a lost dog who has ID tags on his collar; it tells the person that this is somebody's pet rather than a stray. This is the easiest and fastest method of identification provided that the tags stay on the collar and the collar stays on the dog.

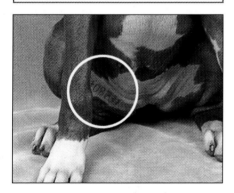

separated from you. If this unfortunate event should occur, the first thing on your mind will be finding him. Proper identification will increase the chances of his being returned to you safely and quickly.

DID YOU KNOW?

As purebred dogs become more and more expensive, especially those of high quality for showing and/or breeding, they have a greater chance of being stolen. The usual collar dog tag is, of course, easily removed. But there are two techniques which are becoming widely utilised for identification.

The puppy microchip implantation involves the injection of a small microchip, about the size of a corn kernel, under the skin of the dog. If your dog shows up at a clinic or shelter, or is offered for resale under less than savory circumstances, it can be positively identified by the microchip. The microchip is scanned and a registry quickly identifies you as the owner. This is not only protection against theft, but should the dog run away or go chasing a varmint and get lost, you have a fair chance of getting it back.

Tattooing is done on various parts of the dog, from its belly to its cheeks. The number tattooed can be your telephone number or any other number which you can easily memorise. When professional dog thieves see a tattooed dog, they usually lose interest in it. Both microchipping and tattooing can be done at your local veterinary clinic. For the safety of our dogs, no laboratory facility or dog broker will accept a tattooed dog as stock.

Tattoos are recommended for identifying your dog. The tattoo is usually located inside the rear thigh. Thieves rarely steal a tattooed dog and, should the dog become lost, a finder can always use the tattoo to locate the owner. The more usual form of identification is, of course, the typical dog tags attached to the collar.

A Boxer MUST be trained. An undisciplined Boxer is simply not enjoyable as a house pet. The more highly trained, the more you will enjoy your dog. Invest time when he is still young and you will reap the benefits for the life of the dog.

Housebreaking and Training Your Boxer

Living with an untrained dog is a lot like owning a piano that you do not know how to play—it is a nice object to look at but it does not do much more than that to bring you pleasure. Now try taking piano lessons and suddenly the piano comes alive and brings forth magical sounds and rhythms that set your heart singing and your body swaying.

The same is true with your Boxer. At first you enjoy seeing him around the house. He does not do much with you other than to need food, water and exercise. Come to think of it, he does not bring you much joy, either. He is a big responsibility with a very small return. And often, he develops unacceptable behaviours that annoy and/or infuriate you to say nothing of bad habits that may end up costing you great sums of money. Not a good thing!

Now train your Boxer. Enroll in an obedience class. Teach him good manners as you learn how and why he behaves the way he does. Find out how to communicate with your dog and how to recognise and understand his communications with you.

Some owners love Boxers so much they buy a new dog every year! Obviously the dogs must be housebroken and trained; an easily cleaned tile floor helps during the training period.

Suddenly the dog takes on a new role in your life—he is smart, interesting, well behaved and fun to be with, and he demonstrates his bond of devotion to you daily. In other words, your Boxer does wonders for your ego because he constantly reminds you that you are not only his leader, you are his hero! Miraculous things have

Puppies are naturally curious and exuberant.

happened—you have a wonderful dog (even your family and friends have noticed the transformation!) and you feel good about yourself.

Those involved with teaching dog obedience and counselling owners about their dogs' behaviour have discovered some interesting facts about dog ownership. For example, training dogs when they are puppies results in the highest rate of success in developing well-mannered and well-adjusted adult dogs. Training an older dog, say from six months to six years of age, can produce almost equal results providing that the owner accepts the dog's slower rate of learning capability and is willing to work patiently to help the dog succeed at developing to his fullest potential. Unfortunately, the patience factor is what many owners of untrained adult dogs lack, so they do not persist until their dogs are successful at learning particular behaviours.

Training a puppy, for example, aged 8 to 16 weeks (20

Training never stops. Boxers must have their early training reinforced continuously. Jumping up to show their affection can become annoying.

weeks at the most) is like working with a dry sponge in a pool of water. The pup soaks up whatever you show him and constantly looks for more things to do and learn. At this early age, his body is not yet producing hormones, and therein lies the reason for such a high rate of success. Without hormones, he is focused on his owners and not particularly interested in investigating other places, dogs, people, etc. You are his leader; his provider of food, water, shelter and security. Therefore, he latches onto you

and wants to stay close. He will usually follow you from room to room, will not let you out of his sight when you are outdoors with him, and respond in like manner to the people and animals you encounter. If, for example, you greet a friend warmly, he will be happy to greet the person as well. If, however, you are hesitant, even anxious, about the approach of a stranger, he will respond accordingly.

Once the puppy begins to produce hormones, his natural curiosity emerges and he begins to investigate the world around him. It is at that time when you may notice that the untrained dog begins to wander away from you and even ignore your commands to stay close. When this behaviour becomes a problem, the owner has two choices: get rid of the dog or train him. It is strongly urged that you choose the latter option.

Occasionally there are no classes available within a reasonable distance from the owner's home. Sometimes there are classes available but the tuition is too costly. Whatever the circumstances, the solution to the problem of lack of lesson availability lies within the pages of this book.

This chapter is devoted to helping you train your Boxer at home. If the recommended procedures are followed faithfully, you may expect positive results

DID YOU KNOW?
If you have other pets in the home and/or interact often with the pets of friends and other family members, your pup will respond to those pets in much the same manner as you do. It is only when you show fear or resentment toward another animal that he will act fearful or unfriendly.

that will prove rewarding to both you and your dog.

Whether your Boxer is a puppy or a mature adult, the methods of teaching and the techniques we use in training basic behaviours are the same. After all, no dog, whether puppy or adult, likes harsh or inhumane methods. All creatures, however, respond favourably to gentle motivational methods and sincere praise and encouragement. Now let us get started.

HOUSEBREAKING

You can train a puppy to relieve itself wherever you choose. For example, city dwellers often train their puppies to relieve themselves in the gutter because large plots of grass are not readily available. Suburbanites, on the other hand, usually have gardens to accommodate their dogs' needs.

Outdoor training includes such surfaces as grass, dirt and cement. Indoor training usually means training your dog to newspaper.

You owe your Boxer decent housing. If, however, you have a large, growing family of Boxers, the pack of Boxers may take over the house and select their own 'bedroom.'

When deciding on the surface and location that you will want your Boxer to use, be sure it is going to be permanent. Training your dog to grass and then changing your mind two months later is extremely difficult for both dog and owner.

Next, choose the command you will use each and every time you want your puppy to void. 'Go hurry up' and 'Go make' are examples of commands commonly used by dog owners.

Get in the habit of asking the puppy, 'Do you want to go hurry up?' (or whatever your chosen relief command is) before you take him out. That way, when he becomes an adult, you will be able to determine if he wants to go out when you ask him. A confirmation will be signs of interest, wagging his tail, watching you intently, going to the door, etc.

PUPPY'S NEEDS
Puppy needs to relieve himself after play periods, after each meal, after he has been sleeping and any time he indicates that he is looking for a place to urinate or defecate.

The urinary and intestinal tract muscles of very young puppies are not fully developed. Therefore, like human babies, puppies need to relieve themselves frequently.

Take your puppy out often— every hour for an eight-week-old, for example. The older the puppy, the less often he will need to relieve himself. Finally, as a mature healthy adult, he will require only three to five relief trips per day.

HOUSING
Since the types of housing and control you provide for your puppy has a direct relationship on the success of housetraining, we consider the various aspects of both before we begin training.

Bringing a new puppy home

DID YOU KNOW?

A basic obedience beginner's class usually lasts for six to eight weeks. Dog and owner attend an hour-long lesson once a week and practice for a few minutes, several times a day, each day at home. If done properly, the whole procedure will result in a well-mannered dog and an owner who delights in living with a pet that is eager to please and enjoys doing things with his owner.

Canine Development Schedule

It is important to understand how and at what age a puppy develops into adulthood. If you are a puppy owner, consult the following Canine Development Schedule to determine the stage of development your Boxer puppy is currently experiencing. This knowledge will help you as you work with the puppy in the weeks and months ahead.

Period	Age	Characteristics
FIRST TO THIRD	**BIRTH TO SEVEN WEEKS**	Puppy needs food, sleep and warmth, and responds to simple and gentle touching. Needs mother for security and disciplining. Needs litter mates for learning and interacting with other dogs. Pup learns to function within a pack and learns pack order of dominance. Begin socialising with adults and children for short periods. Begins to become aware of its environment.
FOURTH	**EIGHT TO TWELVE WEEKS**	Brain is fully developed. Needs socialising with outside world. Remove from mother and littermates. Needs to change from canine pack to human pack. Human dominance necessary. Fear period occurs between 8 and 16 weeks. Avoid fright and pain.
FIFTH	**THIRTEEN TO SIXTEEN WEEKS**	Training and formal obedience should begin. Less association with other dogs, more with people, places, situations. Period will pass easily if you remember this is pup's change-to-adolescence time. Be firm and fair. Flight instinct prominent. Permissiveness and over-disciplining can do permanent damage. Praise for good behaviour.
JUVENILE	**FOUR TO EIGHT MONTHS**	Another fear period about 7 to 8 months of age. It passes quickly, but be cautious of fright and pain. Sexual maturity reached. Dominant traits established. Dog should understand sit, down, come and stay by now.

NOTE: THESE ARE APPROXIMATE TIME FRAMES. ALLOW FOR INDIVIDUAL DIFFERENCES IN PUPPIES.

and turning him loose in your house can be compared to turning a child loose in a sports arena and telling the child that the place is all his! The sheer enormity of the place would be too much for him to handle.

Instead, offer the puppy clearly defined areas where he can play, sleep, eat and live. A room of the house where the family gathers is the most obvious choice. Puppies are social animals and need to feel a part of the pack

> **DID YOU KNOW?**
> Most of all, be consistent. Always take your dog to the same location, always use the same command, and always have him on lead when he is in his relief area, unless a fenced-in garden is available.
>
> By following the Success Method, your Boxer puppy will be completely housetrained by the time his muscle and brain development reach maturity. Keep in mind that small breeds usually mature faster than large breeds, but all puppies should be trained by six months of age.

right from the start. Hearing your voice, watching you while you are doing things and smelling you nearby are all positive reinforcers that he is now a member of your pack. Usually a family room, the kitchen or a nearby adjoining breakfast nook is ideal for provid-

ing safety and security for both puppy and owner.

Within that room there should be a smaller area which the puppy can call his own. A cubbyhole, a wire or fibreglass dog crate or a fenced (not boarded!) corner from which he can view the activities of his new family will be fine. The size of the area or crate is the key factor here. The area must be large enough for the puppy to lay down and stretch out as well as stand up without rubbing his head on the top, yet small enough so that he cannot relieve himself at one end and sleep at the other without coming into contact with his droppings.

Dogs are, by nature, clean animals and will not remain close to their relief areas unless forced to do so. In those cases, they then become dirty dogs and usually remain that way for life.

The crate or cubby should be lined with a clean towel and offer one toy, no more. Do not put food or water in the crate, as eating and drinking will activate his digestive processes and ultimately defeat your purpose as well as make the puppy very uncomfortable as he attempts to 'hold it.'

CONTROL

By control, we mean helping the puppy to create a lifestyle pattern that will be compatible to that of his human pack (YOU!). Just as we guide little children to learn our way of life, we must show the puppy when it is time to play, eat, sleep, exercise and even entertain himself.

he should be crated. Puppies are chewers. They cannot tell the difference between lamp cords, television wires, shoes, table legs, etc. Chewing into a television wire, for example, can be fatal to the puppy while a shorted wire can start a fire in the house.

If the puppy chews on the arm of the chair when he is

This eight-week-old puppy simply cannot figure out this situation. Puppies should not be exposed to frightening experiences as it may imprint them for life.

Your puppy should always sleep in his crate. He should also learn that, during times of household confusion and excessive human activity such as at breakfast when family members are preparing for the day, he can play by himself in relative safety and comfort in his crate. Each time you leave the puppy alone,

alone, you will probably discipline him angrily when you get home. Thus, he makes the association that your coming home means he is going to be hit or punished. (He will not remember chewing up the chair and is incapable of making the association of the discipline with his naughty deed.)

Other times of excitement, such as family parties, etc., can be fun for the puppy providing he can view the activities from the security of his crate. He is not underfoot and he is not being fed all sorts of titbits that will probably cause him stomach distress, yet he still feels a part of the fun.

SCHEDULE

As stated earlier, a puppy should be taken to his relief area each time he is released from his crate, after meals, after a play session, when he first awakens in the morning (at age 8 weeks, this can mean 5 a.m.!) and whenever he indicates by circling or sniffing busily that he needs to urinate or defecate. For a puppy less than ten weeks of age, a routine of taking him out every hour is necessary. As the puppy grows, he will be able to wait for longer periods of time.

Keep trips to his relief area short. Stay no more than five or six minutes and then return to the house. If he goes during that time, praise him lavishly and take him indoors immediately. If he does not, but he has an accident when you go back indoors, pick him up immediately, say 'No! No!' and return to his relief area. Wait a few minutes, then return to the house again. NEVER hit a puppy or rub his face in urine or excrement when he has an accident!

Once indoors, put the puppy in his crate until you have had time to clean up his accident. Then release him to the family area and watch him more closely than before. Chances are, his accident was a result of your not picking up his signal or waiting too long before offering him the opportunity to relieve himself. NEVER hold a grudge against the puppy for accidents.

Let the puppy learn that going outdoors means it is time to relieve himself, not play. Once trained, he will be able to play indoors and out and still differentiate between the times for play versus the times for relief.

Help him develop regular hours for naps, being alone, playing by himself and just resting, all in his crate. Encourage him to entertain himself while you are busy with your activities. Let him learn that having you near is comforting, but it is not your main purpose in life to provide him with undivided attention.

Each time you put a puppy in his crate tell him, 'Crate time!' (or whatever command you choose). Soon, he will run to his crate when he hears you say those words.

In the beginning of his training, do not leave him in his crate for prolonged periods of time except during the night when everyone is sleeping. Make his experience with his crate a pleasant one and, as an adult, he will love his crate and willingly stay in it for several hours. There are millions of people who go to work every day and leave their adult dogs crated while they are away. The dogs accept this as their lifestyle and look forward to 'crate time.'

Crate training provides safety for you, the puppy and the home. It also provides the puppy with a feeling of security, and that helps the puppy achieve self-confidence and clean habits.

Remember that one of the primary ingredients in housetraining your puppy is control. Regardless of your lifestyle, there will always be occasions when you will need to have a place where your dog can stay and be happy and safe. Crate training is the answer for now and in the future.

In conclusion, a few key elements are really all you need for a successful house and crate training method—consistency, frequency, praise, control and supervision. By following these procedures with a normal, healthy puppy, you and the puppy will soon be past the stage of 'accidents' and ready to move on to a full and rewarding life together.

Male Boxers will mark their territory in a most familiar manner.

ROLES OF DISCIPLINE, REWARD AND PUNISHMENT

Discipline, training one to act in accordance with rules, brings order to life. It is as simple as that. Without discipline, particularly in a group society, chaos reigns supreme and the group will eventually perish. Humans and canines are social animals and need some form of discipline in order to function effectively. They must procure food, protect their home base and their young and reproduce to keep the species going.

If there were no discipline in the lives of social animals, they would eventually die from starvation and/or predation by other stronger animals.

In the case of domestic canines, dogs need discipline in their lives in order to understand how their pack (you and other family members) function and how they must act in order to survive.

A large humane society in a highly populated area recently surveyed dog owners regarding their satisfaction with their relationships with their dogs. People who had trained their dogs were 75% more satisfied with their pets than those who had never trained their dogs.

Dr. Edward Thorndike, a psychologist, established *Thorndike's Theory of Learning*, which states that a behaviour that results in a pleasant event tends to be repeated. A behaviour that results in an unpleasant event tends not to be repeated. It is this theory on which training methods are based today. For example, if you manipulate a dog to perform a specific behaviour and reward him for doing it, he is likely to do it again because he enjoyed the end result.

Occasionally, punishment, a penalty inflicted for an offence, is necessary. The best type of punishment often comes from an outside source. For example, a child is told not to touch the stove because he may get burned. He disobeys and touches the stove. In doing so, he receives a burn. From that time on, he respects the heat of the stove and avoids contact with it. Therefore, a behaviour that results in an unpleasant event tends not to be repeated.

A good example of a dog learning the hard way is the dog who chases the house cat. He is told many times to leave the cat alone, yet he persists in teasing the cat. Then, one day he begins chasing the cat but the cat turns and swipes a claw across the dog's face, leaving him with a painful gash on his nose. The final result is that the dog stops chasing the cat.

TRAINING EQUIPMENT
COLLAR

A simple buckle collar is fine for most dogs. One who pulls mightily on the leash may require a chain choker collar. Only in the most severe cases of a dog being totally out of control is it recommended to use a prong or pinch collar, only if these and in this case only if the owner has been instructed in the proper use of such equipment. In some areas, such as the United Kingdom, these types of collars are not allowed.

DID YOU KNOW?

The puppy should also have regular play and exercise sessions when he is with you or a family member. Exercise for a very young puppy can consist of a short walk around the house or garden. Playing can include fetching games with a large ball or an old sock with a knot tied in the middle. (All puppies teethe and need soft things upon which to chew.) Remember to restrict play periods to indoors within his living area (the family room for example) until he is completely housetrained.

THE SUCCESS METHOD
6 Steps to Successful Crate Training

1 Tell the puppy 'Crate time!' and place him in the crate with a small treat (a piece of cheese or half of a biscuit). Let him stay in the crate for five minutes while you are in the same room. Then release him and praise lavishly. Never release him when he is fussing. Wait until he is quiet before you let him out.

2 Repeat Step 1 several times a day.

3 The next day, place the puppy in the crate as before. Let him stay there for ten minutes. Do this several times.

4 Continue building time in five-minute increments until the puppy stays in his crate for 30 minutes with you in the room. Always take him to his relief area after prolonged periods in his crate.

5 Now go back to Step 1 and let the puppy stay in his crate for five minutes, this time while you are out of the room.

6 Once again, build crate time in five-minute increments with you out of the room. When the puppy will stay willingly in his crate (he may even fall asleep!) for 30 minutes with you out of the room, he will be ready to stay in it for several hours at a time.

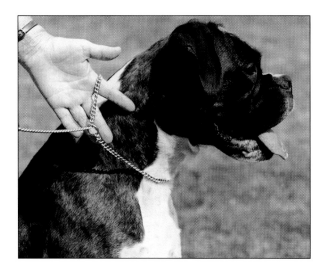

training, rewarding the dog with a food treat away from the table will help him associate praise and the treats with learning new behaviours that obviously please his owner.

TRAINING BEGINS: ASK THE DOG A QUESTION

In order to teach your dog anything, you must first get his attention. After all, he cannot learn anything if he is looking away from you with his mind on something else.

To get his attention, ask him, 'School?' and immediately walk over to him and give him a treat as you tell him 'Good dog.' Wait a minute or two and repeat the routine, this time with a treat in your hand as you approach the dog to within a foot of him. Do not go directly to him, but stop about a foot short of him and hold out the treat as you ask, 'School?' He will see you approaching with a treat in your hand and most likely begin walking toward you. As you meet, give him the treat and praise again.

The third time, ask the question, have a treat in your hand and walk only a short distance toward the dog so that he must walk almost all the way to you. As he reaches you, give him the treat and praise again.

By this time, the dog will probably be getting the idea that if he pays attention to you, especial-

This is the correct way to use a choke chain.

LEAD

A 1- to 2-metre lead is recommended, preferably made of leather, nylon or heavy cloth. A chain lead is not recommended, as many dog owners find that the chain cuts into their hands and that switching the lead back and forth frequently between their hands is painful.

TREATS

Have a bag of treats on hand. Something nutritious and easy to swallow works best; use a soft treat, a chunk of cheese or a piece of cooked chicken rather than a dry biscuit. By the time the dog gets done chewing a dry treat, he will forget why he is being rewarded in the first place! Using food rewards will not teach a dog to beg at the table—the only way to teach a dog to beg at the table is to give him food from the table. In

ly when you ask that question, it will pay off in treats and fun activities for him. In other words, he learns that 'school' means doing fun things with you that result in treats and positive attention for him.

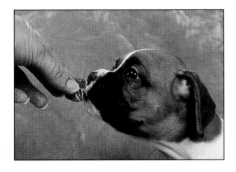

Treats as rewards are used for the most effective Boxer training.

Remember that the dog does not understand your verbal language, he only recognises sounds. Your question translates to a series of sounds for him, and those sounds become the signal to go to you and pay attention; if he does, he will get to interact with you plus receive treats and praise.

THE BASIC COMMANDS
TEACHING SIT
Now that you have the dog's attention, hold the lead in your left hand and the food treat in your right. Place your food hand at the dog's nose and let him lick the treat but not take it from you. Say 'Sit' and slowly raise your food hand from in front of the dog's nose up over his head so that he is looking at the ceiling.

Teaching the Boxer to SIT is one of the easiest commands to accomplish. Therefore, it is wise to use the SIT command as a starting point.

97

As he bends his head upward, he will have to bend his knees to maintain his balance. As he bends his knees, he will assume a sit position. At that point, release the food treat and praise lavishly with comments such as 'Good dog! Good sit!', etc. Remember to always praise enthusiastically, because dogs relish verbal praise from their owners and feel so proud of themselves whenever they accomplish a behaviour.

You will not use food forever in getting the dog to obey your commands. Food is only used to teach new behaviours, and once the dog knows what you want when you give a specific command, you will wean him off of the food treats but still maintain the verbal praise. After all, you will always have your voice with you, but there will be many times when you have no food rewards yet you expect the dog to obey.

TEACHING DOWN

Teaching the down exercise is easy when you understand how the dog perceives the down position, and it is very difficult when you do not. In addition, teaching the down exercise using the wrong method can sometimes make the dog develop such a fear of the down that he either runs away when you say 'down' or he attempts to bite the person who tries to force him down.

Have the dog sit close alongside your left leg, facing in the same direction as you are. Hold the lead in your left hand and a food treat in your right. Now place your left hand lightly on the top of the dog's shoulders where they meet above the spinal cord. Do not push down on the dog's shoulders; simply rest your left hand there so you can guide the dog to lie down close to your left leg rather than to swing away from your side when he drops.

Now place the food hand at the dog's nose, say 'Down' very softly (almost a whisper), and

Do not expect to use a food treat every time you want your dog to obey. Sometimes your Boxer has to be forced to sit when you say SIT.

Three photographs showing the steps in teaching your dog the DOWN exercise. You must instruct the dog properly or your success will be limited.

slowly lower the food hand to the dog's front feet. When the food hand reaches the floor, begin moving it forward along the floor in front of the dog. Keep talking softly to the dog, saying things like, 'Do you want this

Teaching the STAY command in the SIT position.

treat? You can do this, good dog.' Your reassuring tone of voice will help calm the dog as he tries to follow the food hand in order to get the treat.

When the dog's elbows touch the floor, release the food and praise softly. Try to get the dog to

> ### DID YOU KNOW?
>
> If you start with a normal, healthy dog and give him time, patience and some carefully executed lessons, you will reap the rewards of that training for the life of the dog. And what a life it will be! The two of you will find immeasurable pleasure in the companionship you have built together with love, respect and understanding. Good luck and enjoy!

maintain that down position for several seconds before you let him sit up again. The goal here is to get the dog to settle down and not feel threatened in the down position.

TEACHING STAY

It is easy to teach the dog to stay in either a sit or a down position. Again, we use food and praise during the teaching process as we help the dog to understand exactly what it is that we are expecting him to do.

To teach the sit/stay, start with the dog sitting on your left side as before and hold the lead in your

Teaching the STAY command in the DOWN position.

left hand. Have a food treat in your right hand and place your food hand at the dog's nose. Say 'Stay' and step out on your right foot to stand directly in front of the dog, toe to toe, as he licks and nibbles the treat. Be sure to keep his head facing upward to maintain the sit position. Count to five and then swing around to stand next to the dog again with him on your left. As soon as you get back to the original position, release the food and praise lavishly.

To teach the down/stay, do the down as previously described. As soon as the dog lies down, say 'Stay' and step out on your right foot just as you did in the sit/stay. Count to five and then return to

stand beside the dog with him on your left side. Release the treat and praise as always.

Within a week or ten days, you can begin to add a bit of distance between you and your dog when you leave him. When you do, use your left hand open with the palm facing the dog as a stay signal, much the same as the hand signal a police officer uses to stop traffic at an intersection. Hold the food treat in your right hand as before, but this time the food is not touching the dog's nose. He will watch the food hand and quickly learn that he is going to get that treat as soon as you return to his side.

When you can stand 1 metre away from your dog for 30 seconds, you can then begin building time and distance in both stays. Eventually, the dog can be expected to remain in the stay position for prolonged periods of time until you return to him or call him to you. Always praise lavishly when he stays.

Teaching Come

If you make teaching 'Come' a fun experience, you should never have a 'student' that does not love the game or that fails to come when called. The secret, it seems, is never to teach the word 'Come.'

At times when an owner most wants his dog to come when called, the owner is likely upset or anxious and he allows these

> **DID YOU KNOW?**
> When calling the dog, do not say 'Come.' Say things like, 'Rover, where are you? See if you can find me! I have a cookie for you!' Keep up a constant line of chatter with coaxing sounds and frequent questions such as, 'Where are you?' The dog will learn to follow the sound of your voice to locate you and receive his reward.

feelings to come through in the tone of his voice when he calls his dog. Hearing that desperation in his owner's voice, the dog fears the results of going to him and therefore either disobeys outright or runs in the opposite direction. The secret, therefore, is to teach the dog a game and, when you want him to come to you, simply play the game. It is practically a no-fail solution!

To begin, have several members of your family take a few food treats and each go into a different room in the house. Take turns calling the dog, and each person should celebrate the dog's

Teaching the COME command is an absolutely necessary lesson. The secret is to make it a game.

finding him with a treat and lots of happy praise. When a person calls the dog, he is actually inviting the dog to find him and get a treat as a reward for 'winning.'

A few turns of the 'Where are you?' game and the dog will figure out that everyone is playing the game and that each person has a big celebration awaiting his success at locating them. Once he learns to love the game, simply

Many dogs respond better to their name and a short expression like 'Where are you?'

calling out 'Where are you?' will bring him running from wherever he is when he hears that all-important question.

The come command is recognised as one of the most important things to teach a dog, so it is interesting to note that there are trainers who work with thousands of dogs and never teach the actual word 'Come.' Yet these dogs will race to respond to a person who uses the dog's name followed by 'Where are you?' In one instance, for example, a woman has a 12-year-old compan-

ion dog who went blind, but who never fails to locate her owner when asked, 'Where are you?'

Children particularly love to play this game with their dogs. Children can hide in smaller places like a shower or bathtub, behind a bed or under a table. The dog needs to work a little bit harder to find these hiding places, but when he does he loves to celebrate with a treat and a tussle with a favourite youngster.

TEACHING HEEL
Heeling means that the dog walks beside the owner without pulling. It takes time and patience on the owner's part to succeed at teaching the dog that he (the owner) will not proceed unless the dog is walking calmly beside him. Pulling out ahead on the lead is definitely not acceptable.

Begin with holding the lead in your left hand as the dog sits beside your left leg. Hold the loop end of the lead in your right hand but keep your left hand short on the lead so it keeps the dog in close next to you.

Say 'Heel' and step forward on your left foot. Keep the dog close to you and take three steps. Stop and have the dog sit next to you in what we now call the 'heel position.' Praise verbally, but do not touch the dog. Hesitate a moment and begin again with 'Heel,' taking three steps and stopping, at which point the dog is told to sit again.

DID YOU KNOW?

If you begin teaching the heel by taking long walks and letting the dog pull you along, he misinterprets this action as an acceptable form of taking a walk. When you pull back on the lead to counteract his pulling, he reads that tug as a signal to pull even harder!

Your goal here is to have the dog walk those three steps without pulling on the lead. When he will walk calmly beside you for three steps without pulling, increase the number of steps you take to five. When he will walk politely beside you while you take five steps, you can increase the length of your walk to ten steps. Keep increasing the length of your stroll until the dog will walk quietly beside you without pulling as long as you want him to heel. When you stop heeling, indicate to the dog that the exercise is over by verbally praising as you pet him and say 'OK, good dog.' The 'OK' is used as a release word meaning that the exercise is finished and the dog is free to relax.

If you are dealing with a dog who insists on pulling you around, simply 'put on your brakes' and stand your ground until the dog realises that the two of you are not going anywhere until he is beside you and moving at your pace, not his. It may take some time just standing there to convince the dog that you are the leader and you will be the one to decide on the direction and speed of your travel.

Each time the dog looks up at you or slows down to give a slack lead between the two of you, quietly praise him and say, 'Good heel. Good dog.' Eventually, the dog will begin to respond and within a few days he will be walking politely beside you without pulling on the lead. At first, the training sessions should be kept short and very positive; soon the dog will be able to walk nicely with you for increasingly longer distances. Remember also to give the dog free time and the

There is nothing so pitiful as watching a Boxer drag his master down the street because the dog was never trained to heel.

opportunity to run and play when you are done with heel practice.

WEANING OFF FOOD IN TRAINING
Food is used in training new behaviours, yet once the dog understands what behaviour goes with a specific command, it is time to start weaning him off the food treats. At first, give a treat after each exercise. Then, start to give a treat only after every other exercise. Mix up the times when you offer a food reward and the times when you only offer praise so that the dog will never know when he is going to receive both food and praise and when he is going to receive only praise. This is called a variable ratio reward system and it proves successful because there is always the chance that the owner will

produce a treat, so the dog never stops trying for that reward. No matter what, ALWAYS give verbal praise.

OBEDIENCE CLASSES
As previously discussed, it is a good idea to enroll in an obedience class if one is available in your area. Many areas have dog clubs that offer basic obedience training as well as preparatory classes for obedience competition. There are also local dog trainers who offer similar classes.

At obedience trials, dogs can earn titles at various levels of competition. The beginning levels of competition include basic behaviours such as sit, down, heel, etc. The more advanced levels of competition include jumping, retrieving, scent discrimination and signal work. The advanced levels require a dog and owner to put a lot of time and effort into their training; the titles that can be earned at these levels of competition are very prestigious.

OTHER ACTIVITIES FOR LIFE
Whether a dog is trained in the structured environment of a class or alone with his owner at home, there are many activities that can bring fun and rewards to both owner and dog once they have mastered basic control.

Teaching the dog to help out around the home, in the garden

DID YOU KNOW?
Occasionally, a dog and owner who have not attended formal classes have been able to earn entry-level titles by obtaining competition rules and regulations from a local kennel club and practising on their own to a degree of perfection. Obtaining the higher level titles, however, almost always requires extensive training under the tutelage of experienced instructors. In addition, the more difficult levels require more specialised equipment whereas the lower levels do not.

or on the farm provides great satisfaction to both dog and owner. In addition, the dog's help makes life a little easier for his owner and raises his stature as a valued companion to his family. It helps give the dog a purpose; it helps to keep his mind occupied and provides an outlet for his energy.

Backpacking is an exciting and healthful activity that the dog can be taught without assistance from more than his owner. The exercise of walking and climbing is good for man and dog alike, and the bond that they develop together is priceless.

If you are interested in participating in organised competition with your Boxer, there are other activities other than obedience in which you and your dog can become involved. Agility is a popular and fun sport where dogs run through an obstacle course that includes various jumps, tunnels and other exercises to test the dog's speed and coordination. The owners often run through the course beside their dogs to give commands and to guide them through the course. Although competitive, the focus is on fun—it's fun to do and fun to watch, as well as great exercise.

Boxers are very intelligent dogs. When properly maintained and exercised, they can perform many feats of physical splendour.

As a Boxer owner, you have the opportunity to participate in Schutzhund competition if you choose. Schutzhund originated as a test to determine the best quality Boxers to be used for breeding stock. It is now used as a way to evaluate working ability and temperament, and some Boxer owners choose to train and compete with their dogs in Schutzhund trials. There are three levels of Schutzhund, SchH. I, SchH. II and SchH. III, each level being progressively more difficult to complete successfully. Each level consists of training, obedience and protection phases. Training for Schutzhund is intense and must be practised consistently to keep the dog keen. The experience of Schutzhund training is very rewarding for dog and owner, and the Boxer's tractability is well suited for this type of training.

105

Health Care
of Your Boxer

Dogs, being mammals like human beings, suffer many of the same physical illnesses as people. They might even share many of the psychological problems. Since people usually know more about human diseases than canine maladies, many of the terms used in this chapter will be the familiar terms, not necessarily those used by veterinary surgeons. We'll still use the term X-RAY, instead of the more acceptable term RADI-OGRAPH. We will also use the familiar term SYMPTOMS even though dogs don't have symptoms, dogs have CLINICAL SIGNS. SYMPTOMS, by the way, are verbal descriptions of the patient's feelings. Since dogs can't speak, we have to look for clinical signs...but we still use the term SYMPTOMS in this book.

As a general rule, medicine is PRACTISED. That term is not arbitrary. Medicine is an art. It is a constantly changing art as we learn more and more about genetics, electronic aids (like CAT scans) and opinions. There are many dog maladies, like canine hip dysplasia, which are not universally treated in the same manner. Some veterinary surgeons opt for surgery more often than others.

You have a responsibility to your Boxer to keep him healthy. Regular visits to your local veterinary surgeon will inhibit debilitating diseases and keep your dog free of parasites, both internal and external.

SELECTING A VETERINARY SURGEON

Your selection of a veterinary surgeon should not be based upon personality (as most are) but upon their convenience to your home. You want a doctor who is close as you might have emergencies or multiple visits for treatments. You want a doctor who has services that you might require such as a boarding kennel, grooming facilities, who makes sophisticated pet supplies available and who has a good reputation for ability and responsiveness. There is nothing more frustrating than having to wait a day or more to get a response from a veterinary surgeon.

All veterinary surgeons are licensed and their diplomas and/or certificates should be displayed in their waiting rooms. There are, however, many veterinary specialties which usually require further studies and internships. There are specialists in heart problems (veterinary cardiologists), skin problems (veterinary dermatologists), teeth and gum problems (veterinary dentists), eye problems (veterinary ophthalmologists), x-rays (veterinary radiologists), and surgeons who have specialties in bones, muscles or other organs. Most veterinary surgeons do routine surgery such as neutering, stitching up wounds and dock-

ing tails for those breeds in which such is required for show purposes. When the problem affecting your dog is serious, it is not unusual or impudent to get another medical opinion. You might also want to compare costs between several veterinary surgeons. Sophisticated health care and veterinary services can be very costly. Don't be bashful to discuss these costs with your veterinary surgeon or his (her) staff. It is not infrequent that important decisions are based upon financial considerations.

Your veterinary surgeon can easily be your dog's most VALUABLE friend.

PREVENTATIVE MEDICINE

It is much easier, less costly and more effective to practice preventative medicine than to fight bouts of illness and disease.

Properly bred puppies come from parents that were selected based upon their genetic disease profile. Their mothers should have been vaccinated, free of all internal and external parasites, and properly nourished. For these reasons, a visit to the veterinary surgeon who cared for the dam (mother) is recommended. The dam can pass on disease resistance to her puppies. This resistance can last for 8-10 weeks. She can also pass on parasites and many infections. That's why you should visit the veterinary surgeon who cared for the dam.

WEANING TO FIVE MONTHS OLD

Puppies should be weaned by the time they are about two months old. A puppy that remains for at least eight weeks with its mother and litter mates usually adapts better to other

When a vet or breeder examines a Boxer puppy, he can expect lots of kisses. Licking is part of being a dog!

dogs and people later in its life.

In every case, you should have your newly acquired puppy examined by a veterinary surgeon immediately. Vaccination programmes usually begin when the puppy is very young.

The puppy will have its teeth examined, have its skeletal conformation checked, and have its general health checked prior to certification by the veterinary surgeon. Many puppies have problems with their knee caps, eye cataracts and other eye problems, heart murmurs and undescended testicles. They may also have personality problems and your veterinary surgeon might have training in temperament evaluation.

VACCINATION SCHEDULING

Most vaccinations are given by injection and should only be done by a veterinary surgeon. Both he and you should keep a record of the date of the injection, the identification of the vaccine and the amount given. The vaccination scheduling is based on a 15-day cycle. The

HEALTH AND VACCINATION SCHEDULE

Age in Weeks:	3rd	6th	8th	10th	12th	14th	16th	20-24th
Worm Control	✔	✔	✔	✔	✔	✔	✔	✔
Neutering								✔
Heartworm*		✔						✔
Parvovirus		✔		✔		✔		✔
Distemper			✔		✔		✔	
Hepatitis			✔		✔		✔	
Leptospirosis		✔		✔		✔		
Parainfluenza		✔		✔		✔		
Dental Examination			✔					✔
Complete Physical			✔					✔
Temperament Testing			✔					
Coronavirus					✔			
Canine Cough		✔						
Hip Dysplasia							✔	
Rabies*								✔

Vaccinations are not instantly effective. It takes about two weeks for the dog's immune system to develop antibodies. Most vaccinations require annual booster shots. Your veterinary surgeon should guide you in this regard.
*Not applicable in the United Kingdom

first vaccinations should start when the puppy is 6-8 weeks old, then 15 days later when it is 10-12 weeks of age and later when it is 14-16 weeks of age. Vaccinations should NEVER be given without a 15-day lapse between injections. Most vaccinations immunise your puppy against viruses.

The usual vaccines contain immunising doses of several different viruses such as distemper, parvovirus, parainfluenza and hepatitis. There are other vaccines available when the puppy is at risk. You should rely upon

DID YOU KNOW?

Caring for the puppy starts before the puppy is born by keeping the dam healthy and well-nourished. When the puppy is about three weeks old, it must start its disease-control regimen. The first treatments will be for worms. Most puppies have worms, even if they are tested negative for worms. The test essentially is checking the stool specimens for the eggs of the worms. The worms continually shed eggs except during their dormant stage when they just rest in the tissues of the puppy. During this stage they don't shed eggs and are not evident during a routine examination.

professional advice. This is especially true for the booster shot programme. Most vaccination programmes require a booster when the puppy is a year old, and once a year thereafter. In some cases, circumstances may require more frequent immunisations.

Canine cough, more formally known as tracheobronchitis, is treated with a vaccine which is sprayed into the dog's nostrils.

The effectiveness of a parvovirus vaccination programme can be tested to be certain that the vaccinations are protective. Your veterinary surgeon will explain and manage all of these details.

You should examine your dog's teeth and gums regularly. Rely on your vet's opinion about professional dental care to maintain your Boxer's dental health. Doggie breath often indicates a dental or other medical problem.

FIVE MONTHS TO ONE YEAR OF AGE
By the time your puppy is five months old, he should have completed his vaccination programme. During his physical

DID YOU KNOW?

A dental examination is in order when the dog is between six months and one year of age and any permanent teeth that have erupted incorrectly can be corrected. It is important to begin a brushing regimen, preferably using a two-sided brushing technique, whereby both sides of the tooth are brushed at the same time. Durable nylon and safe edible chews should be a part of your puppy's arsenal for good health, good teeth and pleasant breath. The vast majority of dogs three to four years old and older has diseases of their gums from lack of dental attention. Using the various types of dental chews can be very effective in controlling dental plaque.

By the time your dog is a year old, you should have become very comfortable with your local veterinary surgeon and have agreed on scheduled visits for booster vaccinations. Blood tests should now be taken regularly, for comparative purposes, for such variables as cholesterol and triglyceride levels, thyroid hormones, liver enzymes, blood cell counts, etc.

The eyes, ears, nose and throat should be examined regularly and annual cleaning of the teeth is a ritual. For teeth scaling, the dog must be anaesthetised.

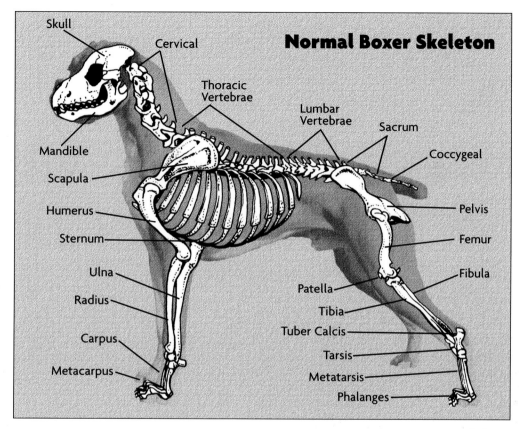

Normal Boxer Skeleton

Skull, Cervical, Thoracic Vertebrae, Lumbar Vertebrae, Sacrum, Coccygeal, Mandible, Scapula, Humerus, Sternum, Ulna, Radius, Carpus, Metacarpus, Patella, Tibia, Tuber Calcis, Tarsis, Metatarsis, Phalanges, Pelvis, Femur, Fibula

examination he should be evaluated for the common hip dysplasia plus other diseases of the joints. There are tests to assist in the prediction of these problems. Other tests can also be run, such as the parvovirus antibody titer, which can assess the effectiveness of the vaccination programme.

Unless you intend to breed or show your dog, neutering the puppy at six months of age is recommended. Discuss this with your veterinary surgeon.

By the time your Boxer is seven or eight months of age, he can be seriously evaluated for his conformation to the club standard, thus determining his show potential and hisdesirability as a sire (or a dam). If the puppy is not top class and therefore is not a candidate for a serious breeding programme, most professionals advise neutering the puppy. Neutering has proven to be extremely beneficial to both male and female puppies. Besides the obvious impossibili-

In order for your dog to perform strenuous exercises, he must be in top physical condition.

ty of pregnancy, it inhibits (but does not prevent) breast cancer in bitches and prostate cancer in male dogs.

Outside Britain, blood tests are performed for heartworm infestation and it is possible that your puppy will be placed on a preventative therapy which will prevent heartworm infection as

Disease	What is it?	What causes it?	Symptoms
Leptospirosis	Severe disease that affects the internal organs; can be spread to people.	A bacterium, which is often carried by rodents, that enters through mucous membranes and spreads quickly throughout the body.	Range from fever, vomiting and loss of appetite in less severe cases to shock, irreversible kidney damage and possibly death in most severe cases.
Rabies	Potentially deadly virus that infects warm-blooded mammals. Not seen in United Kingdom.	A bacterium, which is often carried by rodents, that enters through mucous membranes and spreads quickly throughout the body.	1st stage: dog exhibits change in behaviour, fear. 2nd stage: dog's behaviour becomes more aggressive. 3rd stage: loss of coordination, trouble with bodily functions.
Parvovirus	Highly contagious virus, potentially deadly.	Ingestion of the virus, which is usually spread through the faeces of infected dogs.	Most common: severe diarrhoea. Also vomiting, fatigue, lack of appetite.
Kennel cough	Contagious respiratory infection.	Combination of types of bacteria and virus. Most common: *Bordetella bronchiseptica* bacteria and parainfluenza virus.	Chronic cough.
Distemper	Disease primarily affecting respiratory and nervous system.	Virus that is related to the human measles virus.	Mild symptoms such as fever, lack of appetite and mucous secretion progress to evidence of brain damage, 'hard pad.'
Hepatitis	Virus primarily affecting the liver.	Canine adenovirus type I (CAV-1). Enters system when dog breathes in particles.	Lesser symptoms include listlessness, diarrhoea, vomiting. More severe symptoms include 'blue-eye' (clumps of virus in eye).
Coronavirus	Virus resulting in digestive problems.	Virus is spread through infected dog's faeces.	Stomach upset evidenced by lack of appetite, vomiting, diarrhoea.

well as control other internal parasites.

DOGS OLDER THAN ONE YEAR

Continue to visit the veterinary surgeon at least once a year. There is no such disease as old age, but bodily functions do change with age, and the eyes and ears are no longer as efficient. Neither are the internal workings of the liver, kidneys and intestines. Proper dietary changes, recommended by your veterinary surgeon, can make life more pleasant for the aging Boxer and you.

BREED-SPECIFIC HEALTH PROBLEMS OF THE BOXER

Before we consider the various hereditary and congenital diseases that the Boxer is prone to, let's talk about your responsibility in keeping your Boxer healthy. How much does your Boxer love you? This question is not meant to stir your romantic imagination. Instead we are calling upon your astute devotion and necessary responsibility to care for your Boxer properly.

Unfortunately there are too many conditions that appear to be prominent in our breed, though the dedication and knowledge of breeders have limited the occurrence of many of these illnesses. For your sake, and the sake of the puppy that you purchase, be certain that the

Your Boxer's health is directly related to the care you give him. Regular veterinary check-ups are a requirement for a sound health care programme.

breeder has done his homework. Screening for the various congenital defects is the first step to ensuring a longer life for the Boxers around us. Breeders that do not feel it is necessary to test their stock are the breeders you want to avoid. Don't let a smooth-talking breeder convince you that his stock is unique and that he has never encountered any problems with his Boxers. What this breeder is really saying is, 'I don't recognise any of those problems' and 'I haven't screened any of my dogs.'

The second step toward a healthy Boxer is your education of the conditions that may affect the Boxer. There are early warning signs in many of these conditions and you should always keep a close eye on your dog.

Perhaps the most disheartening disease that Boxer breeders and owners must contend with is cancer, which of course comes in many forms. Breeders must screen their stock for cancers, though it is difficult to be certain since so much about cancer is still being learned. The breed can be prone to both malignant and benign forms, the most common form of malignant cancer is a mast-cell tumour.

The second condition that Boxers suffer from concerns the heart. The defect known as dilated cardiomyopathy, affecting the heart muscles, causes heart failure in Boxers. Like a balloon, the muscles of the heart become thin and stretched, keeping the heart from functioning properly and pumping blood efficiently. Although cardiomyopathy affects other breeds, in Boxers its genetic predisposition is likely dominant; thereby making it essential for Boxer breeders to screen their stock before breeding. Owners should keep their eyes out for early warning signs that might include general weakness, difficulty breathing, moping, coughing, difficulty with vigorous activity, lack or loss of appetite, increased heart rate and maybe fainting. Veterinary examinations

are essential, because in worst case scenarios there are no signs. This is especially true with our breed. Dilated cardiomyopathy can be positively identified by your vet, and although there is no cure presently, many Boxers respond well to therapies that include dietary supplements.

Less prevalent in the breed is aortic stenosis, another heart condition that involves the aortic valve and its obstruction. It affects young puppies and is genetically transmitted in Boxers.

Bloat claims more lives of Boxers than anyone would like to admit. In fact, purebred dogs in general are three or four times as likely to be affected than are mongrels. This condition, which nevertheless is not believed to be congenital, occurs in deep-chested dogs like the Boxer. Gastric dilatation or volvulus, as bloat is called by veterinary surgeons, refers to the condition in which the stomach fills up with air (which the dog swallows). The stomach then twists, blocking the flow of food, blood, etc., from entering or exiting the organ, and often causing death as toxins are released into the dog's bloodstream. Approximately one-third of the dogs that suffer from bloat do not recover.

While the condition is never entirely avoidable, there are a

Some Boxers, unfortunately, suffer from cancer. Their second most serious condition is heart disease. Only your veterinary surgeon can accurately diagnose these ailments.

number of precautions owners can take to protect their Boxer from bloat. Feed your adult Boxer in three smaller meals per day instead of one large meal, which the dog would have the tendency to gobble up. It is in the gulping of food (and air) that air is swallowed to cause bloat. Some vets recommend adding squeaky toys or chew bones to the dog's bowl so that the dog has to eat around them, and therefore never gulp his food. Add water to dry kibble, and have water available during the day but never at mealtimes. Like the rule your mother told you about swimming as a child, do not let the dog exercise one hour before or after he eats. Use a bowl stand to lift your dog's food so that he does not have to stretch his neck to the floor to eat. If you can get into the habit of enforcing these simple precautions, your Boxer has a better chance of a long, happy, bloat-free life.

As with most other medium- to large-size dogs, Boxers are prone to joint and skeletal problems, the commonest being hip dysplasia. While many Boxers are genetically susceptible to hip dysplasia, not all dogs will show signs of it. Breeders commonly have a dog x-rayed at two years of age, before they are bred, to determine the quality of the dog's hips. Hip dysplasia is not

DO YOU KNOW ABOUT HIP DYSPLASIA?

Hip dysplasia is a fairly common condition found in Boxers, as well as other breeds. When a dog has hip dysplasia, its hind leg has an incorrectly formed hip joint. By constant use of the hip joint, it becomes more and more loose, wears abnormally and may become arthritic.

Hip dysplasia can only be confirmed with an x-ray, but certain symptoms may indicate a problem. Your Boxer may have a hip dysplasia problem if it walks in a peculiar manner, hops instead of smoothly running, uses his hinds legs in unison (to keep the pressure off the weak joint), has trouble getting up from a prone position and always sits with both legs together on one side of its body. As the dog matures, it may adapt well to life with a bad hip, but in a few years the arthritis develops and many Boxers with hip dysplasia become cripples. Hip dysplasia is considered an inherited disease and can usually be diagnosed when the dog is three to nine months old. Some experts claim that a special diet might help your puppy outgrow the bad hip, but the usual treatments are surgical. The removal of the pectineus muscle, the removal of the round part of the femur, reconstructing the pelvis and replacing the hip with an artificial one. All of these surgical interventions are expensive, but they are usually very successful. Follow the advice of your veterinary surgeon.

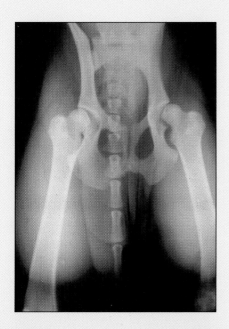

Hip Dysplasia

Compare the two hip joints and you'll understand dysplasia better. Hip dysplasia is a badly worn hip joint caused by improper fit of the bone into the socket. It is easily the most common hip problem in Boxers.

The healthy hip joint on the right and the unhealthy hip joint on the left.

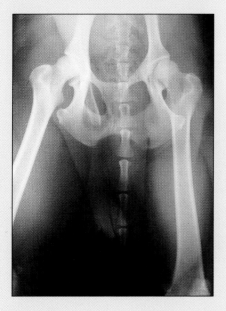

Hip dysplasia can only be positively diagnosed by x-ray. Boxers manifest the problem when they are between four and nine months of age, the so-called fast growth period.

merely a cosmetic smear, a condition that affects the gait of show dogs; it is a serious, crippling disease that can render a beloved pet wracked with pain and lame. Consider how vigorously your Boxer loves to play and jump! Now imagine that every step he takes causes sharp pain throughout his body. No one wants to see his dog unable to run without discomfort. Today there are simply too many irresponsibly bred dogs, dogs whose parents were not screened for dysplasia, who can barely keep up with their owners while walking through the park or on the ocean front.

A similar form of dysplasia concerns the elbows, which affects dogs quite suddenly, rendering them lame. Arthritis usually results in the elbow joints from the complex of disorders that veterinary surgeons call elbow dysplasia. As with hip dysplasia, the dogs are x-rayed for clinical signs of elbow dysplasia. Only dogs that have 'normal' elbows should be used for breeding purposes.

The bleeding disorder known as von Willebrand's disease affects many purebred dogs, including the Boxer. This is an inherited disorder that is believed to be associated with hypothyroidism. While the incidence of von Willebrand's disease has been on the rise in recent years, there are ways of determining the amount of the VW factor in the blood.

Hypothyroidism, a hormonal problem that is fairly common in Boxers, usually shows up in mature dogs, usually no early than five years of age. There are few early signs that an owner

Elbow dysplasia in a three-and-a-half-year-old dog.

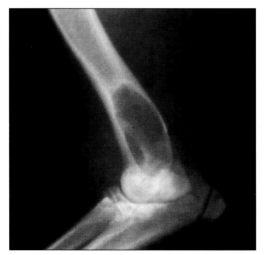
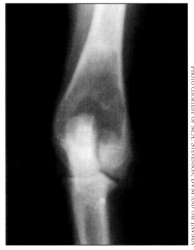

would recognise, though lethargy and recurrent illness or infection have been cited, as has loss of hair. Obesity, often thought to be the most common manifestation, is seen in very few cases. Although the diagnosis of hypothyroidism is tricky, vets can treat the disease rather easily and the expense incurred is not great.

In the early 1980s, England's Boxer population was scourged by progressive axonopathy, an inherited nerve disorder that is seen exclusively in our breed. Thanks to the expertise of animal geneticist Dr. Bruce Cattanach, the mode of inheritance of PA was confirmed. Breeders in England, responsibly breeding away from affected dogs, have completely eradicated the breed from PA. The disease is characterised by awkward rear movement in young pups, usually six months of age, which eventually progresses to the forequarters. Although both parents must carry the genes for PA for the pups to be affected, any carrier dog or its progeny should not be bred.

Another disease that affects the Boxer almost exclusively is known as histiocytic ulcerative colitis. Affecting young dogs less than two years old, this inflammatory disorder of the bowels is marked by diarrhoea and similar signs of colitis. A combination of antibiotics and diet helps to ease sufferers, though there is no cure and the condition is chronic. Since a genetic link is suspected by vets, affects dogs are not to be bred.

There are far too many hereditary conditions that affect the Boxer to describe here. Discuss any of the mentioned diseases with your veterinary surgeon and your breeder. Responsible breeders know their lines in and out and should be able to allay your fears of the possibilities of any of these conditions in your puppy. Amongst the other conditions that veterinary surgeons recommend Boxer folk should look out for are: Cushing's syndrome, corneal ulcers, distichiasis, entropion, lymphosarcoma, and pulmonic stenosis

SKIN PROBLEMS IN BOXERS
Veterinary surgeons are consulted by dog owners for skin problems more than any other group of diseases or maladies. Dogs' skin is almost as sensitive as human skin and both suffer almost the same ailments. (Though the occurrence of acne in dogs is rare!) For this reason, veterinary dermatology has developed into a specialty practised by many veterinary surgeons.

Since many skin problems have visual symptoms which are

almost identical, it requires the skill of an experienced veterinary dermatologist to identify and cure many of the more severe skin disorders. Simply put, if your dog is suffering from a skin disorder, seek professional assistance as quickly as possible. As with all diseases, the earlier a problem is identified and treated, the more successful is the cure.

Pet shops sell many treatments for skin problems. Most of the treatments are simply directed at symptoms and not the underlying problem(s).

INHERITED SKIN PROBLEMS
Many skin disorders are inherited and some are fatal.

Acrodermatitis is an inherited disease which is transmitted by BOTH parents. The parents, which appear (phenotypically) normal, have a recessive gene for acrodermatitis, meaning that they carry, but are not affected by the disease.

Acrodermatitis is just one example of how difficult it is to diagnose and treat many dog diseases. The cost and skills required to ascertain whether two dogs should be mated is too high even though puppies with acrodermatitis rarely reach two years of age.

Other inherited skin problems are usually not as fatal as acrodermatitis. All inherited diseases must be diagnosed and treated by a veterinary specialist. There are active programmes being undertaken by many veterinary pharmaceutical manufacturers to solve most, if not all, of the common skin problems of dogs.

PARASITE BITES
Many of us are allergic to mosquito bites. The bites itch, erupt and may even become infected. Dogs have the same reaction to fleas, ticks and/or mites. When you feel the prick of the mosquito when it bites you, you have a chance to kill it with your hand. Unfortunately, when our dog is bitten by a flea, tick or mite, it can only scratch it away or bite

it. By the time the dog has been bitten, the parasite has done some of its damage. It may also have laid eggs to cause further problems in the near future. The itching from parasite bites is probably due to the saliva injected into the site when the parasite sucks the dog's blood.

ACRAL LICK DISEASE
Boxers and other dogs about the same size (like Labrador Retrievers), have a very poorly understood syndrome called *acral lick.* The manifestation of the problem is the dog's tireless attack at a specific area of the body, almost always the legs. They lick so intensively that they remove the hair and skin leaving an ugly, large wound. There is no absolute cure, but corticosteroids are the most common treatment.

AIRBORNE ALLERGIES
Another interesting allergy is pollen allergy. Humans have hay fever, rose fever and other fevers with which they suffer during the pollinating season. Many dogs suffer the same allergies. So when the pollen count is high, your dog might suffer. Don't expect them to sneeze and have runny noses like humans. Dogs react to pollen allergies the same way they react to fleas—they scratch and bite themselves. Boxers are very susceptible to airborne pollen allergies.

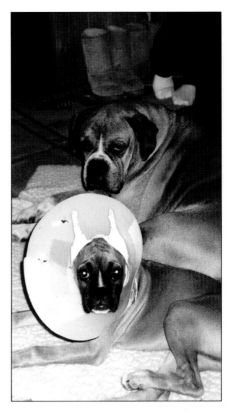

Acral lick results from the Boxer's constant licking at a hot spot on its leg. The area eventually becomes raw. The collar used for a Boxer's healing ears may be helpful in treating acral lick disease. The problem is poorly understood by veterinary surgeons.

Dogs, like humans, can be tested for allergens. Discuss the testing with your veterinary dermatologist.

FOOD ALLERGIES
Dogs are allergic to many foods which are best-sellers and highly recommended by breeders and veterinary surgeons. Changing the brand of food that you buy may not eliminate the problem because the element of the food to which the dog is allergic may also be contained in the new brand.

Recognising a food allergy is difficult. Humans vomit or have rashes when they eat a food to which they are allergic. Dogs neither vomit nor (usually) develop a rash. Instead they itch, scratch and bite, thus making the diagnosis extremely difficult. While pollen allergies and para-site bites are usually seasonal, food allergies are year-round problems.

TREATING FOOD PROBLEMS

Handling food allergies and food intolerance yourself is possible. Put your dog on a diet which it has never had. Obviously if it has never eaten this new food it can't have been allergic or intolerant of it. Start with a single ingredient

> **DID YOU KNOW?**
> Fleas have been around for millions of years and have adapted to changing host animals.
> They are able to go through a complete life cycle in less than one month or they can extend their lives to almost two years by remaining as pupae or cocoons. They do not need blood or any other food for up to 20 months.
> They have been measured as being able to jump 300,000 times and can jump 150 times their length in any direction including straight up. Those are just a few of the reasons they are so successful in infesting a dog!

> **DID YOU KNOW?**
> There are drugs which prevent fleas from maturing from egg to adult.
> The weak link is the maturation from a larva to a pupa.
> Methoprene and fenoxycarb mimic the effect of maturation enhancers, thus, in effect, killing the larva before it pupates.
> Methoprene is mildly effective in killing flea eggs while fenoxy-carb is better able to stand UV rays from the sun. There is a combination of both drugs which has an effective life of 6 months and destroys 93% of the flea population.
> There are desiccants which dry out the eggs, larvae and adult fleas. These desiccants are common, well known and do not usually affect dogs, cats, humans or other mammalian animals.
> Desiccants include silica gel, sodium borate and diatomaceous earth. The best known and most effective is polymerized borate which is marketed by Rx for Fleas Plus® (Fleabusters®).

which is NOT in the dog's diet at the present time. Ingredients like chopped beef or fish are common in dog's diets, so try something more exotic like ostrich, rabbit, pheasant or even just vegetables such as potatoes. Keep the dog on this diet (with no additives) for a month. If the symptoms of food allergy or intolerance disappear, chances are that you have defined the cause.

Don't think that the single ingredient cured the problem. You still must find a suitable diet and ascertain which ingredient in the old diet was objectionable. This is most easily done by adding ingredients to the new diet one at a time until the problem is solved. Let the dog stay on the modified diet for a month before you add another ingredient.

An alternative method is to carefully study the ingredients in the diet to which your dog is allergic or intolerable. Identify the main ingredient in this diet and eliminate the main ingredient by buying a different food which does not have that ingredient. Keep experimenting until the symptoms disappear after one month on the new diet.

EXTERNAL PARASITES

Of all the problems to which dogs are prone, none is more well known and frustrating than fleas. Fleas, which usually refers to fleas, ticks and mites, are relatively simple to cure but difficult to prevent. The opposite is true for the parasites which are harboured inside the body. They are a bit more difficult to cure but they are easier to control.

FLEAS

It is possible to control flea infestation but you have to understand the life cycle of a typical flea in order to control them. Basically fleas are a summertime problem and their

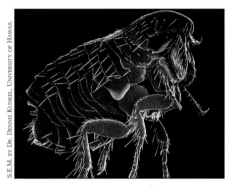

A scanning electron micrograph (SEM) of a dog flea, *Ctenocephalides canis*, magnified about 30x.

S.E.M. BY DR. DENNIS KUNKEL, UNIVERSITY OF HAWAII.

effective treatment (destruction) is environmental. The problem is that there is no single flea control medicine (insecticide) which can be used in every flea infested area. To understand flea control you must apply suitable treatment to the weak link in the life cycle of the flea.

THE LIFE CYCLE OF A FLEA

Fleas are found in four forms: eggs, larvae, pupae and adults. You really need a low-power microscope or hand lens to identify a living flea's eggs, pupae or larva. They spend their whole lives on your Boxer unless they are forcibly removed by brushing, bathing, scratching or biting.

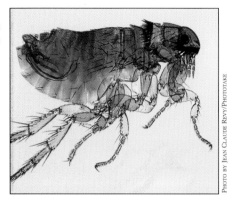

A male dog flea, *Ctenocephalides canis*, magnified about 50x.

PHOTO BY JEAN CLAUDE REVY/PHOTOTAKE

Several species infest both dog and cats. The dog flea is scientifically known as *Ctenocephalides canis* while the cat flea is *Ctenocephalides felis*. Cat fleas are very common on dogs.

Fleas lay eggs while they are in residence on your dog. These eggs do not adhere to the hair of your dog and they simply fall off almost as soon as they dry (they may be a bit damp when initially laid). These eggs are the reservoir of future flea infestations. If your dog scratches himself and is able to dislodge a few fleas,

Dog flea eggs magnified 12x.

they simply fall off and await a future chance to attack a dog...or even a person. Yes, fleas from

Male cat flea, *Ctenocephalides felis*, commonly found on dogs as well as cats.

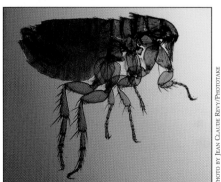

PHOTO BY JEAN CLAUDE REVY/PHOTOTAKE

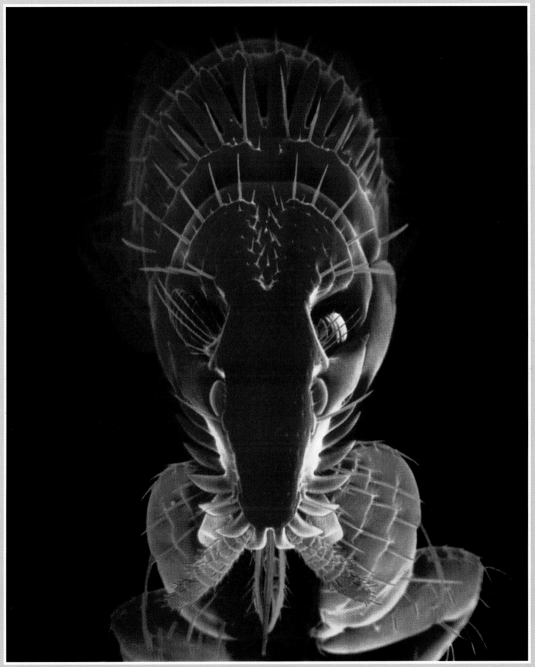

A scanning electron micrograph of a dog or cat flea,
Ctenocephalides, magnified about 100x. The flea has been coloured for effect.

The Life Cycle of the Flea

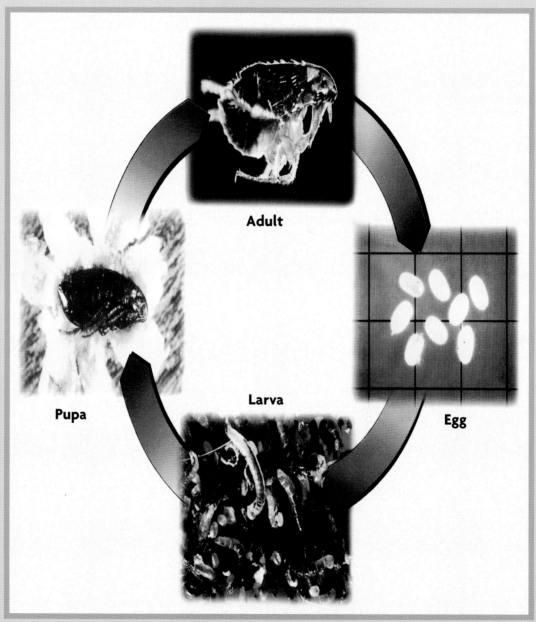

Adult

Pupa

Larva

Egg

The Life Cycle of the Flea was posterized by Fleabusters. Poster courtesy of Fleabusters® Rx for Fleas.

PHOTO BY DWIGHT R. KUHN

must be mopped several times a day. Drops of food onto the floor are actually food for flea larvae! All rugs and furniture must be vacuumed several times a day. Don't forget closets, under furniture, cushions. A study has reported that a vacuum cleaner with a beater bar can only remove 20% of the larvae and 50% of the eggs. The vacuum bags should be discarded into a sealed plastic

Dwight R. Kuhn's wonderful action photo showing a flea jumping from a dog's hair.

Boxers can easily pick up fleas and ticks outdoors.

bag or burned. The vacuum machine itself should be cleaned. The outdoor area to which your dog has access must also be treated with an insecticide.

This all sounds like a lot of work! It is and, therefore, if you

dogs bite people. That's why it is so important to control fleas both on the dog and in the dog's entire environment. You must, therefore, treat the dog and the environment simultaneously.

DE-FLEAING THE HOME
Cleanliness is the simple rule. If you have a cat living with your dog, the matter is more complicated since most dog fleas are actually cat fleas. But since cats climb onto many areas that are never accessible to dogs (like window sills, table tops, etc.), you have to clean all of these areas, too. The hard floor surfaces (tiles, wood, stone and linoleum)

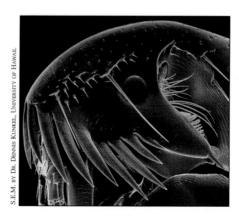

S.E.M. BY DR. DENNIS KUNKEL, UNIVERSITY OF HAWAII.

The head of the dog flea, *Ctenocephalides canis*, magnified about 165x.

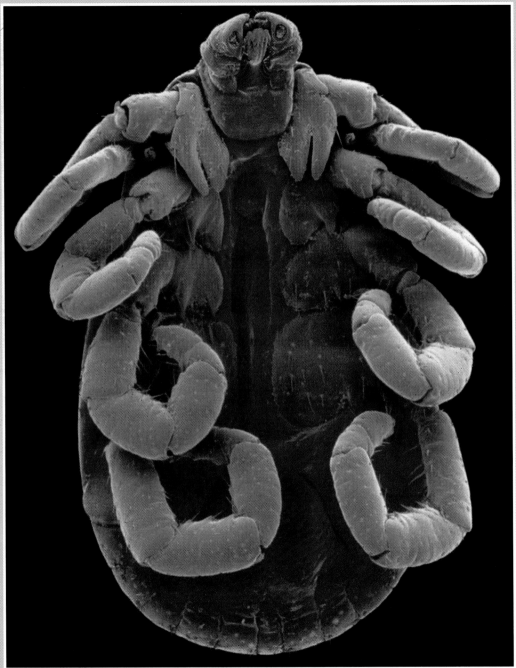

The dog tick, *Dermacentor variabilis*, is the most common tick found on Boxers.
Look at the eight legs! No wonder ticks are difficult to remove.

PHOTO BY DWIGHT R. KUHN

ming bushes, spreading insecticide and being careful not to poison areas in which fishes or other animals reside.

This is best done by an outside service specialising in defleaing. Your vet should be able to recommend a local service.

Human lice look like dog lice; the two are very closely related.

TICKS AND MITES

Though not as common as fleas, ticks and mites are found all over the tropical and temperate world. They don't bite, like fleas, rather they harpoon. They dig their sharp proboscis (nose) into the dog's skin and drink the blood. Their only food and drink is dog's blood. Dogs can get Lyme disease, Rocky Mountain spotted fever (normally found in the U.S. only), paralysis and

can afford it, you are better off hiring a professional to do it.

While there are many drugs available to kill fleas on the dog itself, such as the miracle drug ivermectin, it is best to have the de-fleaing and de-worming supervised by your vet. Ivermectin is effective against many external and internal parasites including heartworms, roundworms, tapeworms, flukes, ticks and mites. It has not been approved for use to control these pests, but veterinary surgeons frequently use it anyway. Ivermectin may not be available in all areas.

Ticks can only live by ingesting blood.

many other diseases, from ticks and mites. They may live where fleas are found except they like to hide in cracks or seams in walls wherever dogs live. They are controlled the same way fleas are controlled.

The dog tick *Dermacentor variabilis* may well be the most common dog tick in many geo-

STERILISING THE ENVIRONMENT

Besides cleaning your home with vacuum cleaners and mops, you have to treat the outdoor range of your dog. This means trim-

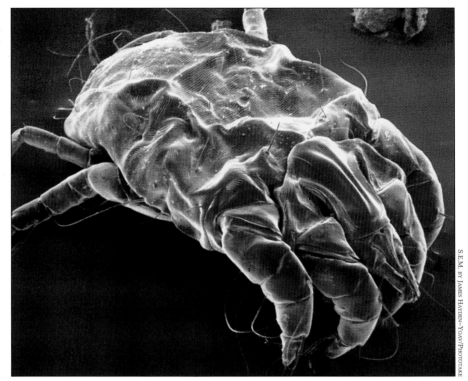

The mange mite, *Psoroptes bovis,* magnified more than 200x.

S.E.M. BY JAMES HAYDEN–YOAV/PHOTOTAKE

graphical areas, especially those areas where the climate is hot and humid.

Most dog ticks have life expectancies of a week to six months, depending upon climatic conditions. They can neither jump nor fly, but they can crawl slowly and can range up to 5 metres (16 feet) to reach a sleeping or unsuspecting dog.

MANGE

Mites cause a skin irritation called mange. Some are contagious, like *Cheyletiella*, ear mites, scabies and chiggers. The

non-contagious mites are *Demodex*. The most serious of the mites is the ear mite infestation. Ear mites are usually controlled with ivermectin.

It is essential that your dog be treated for mange as quickly as possible because some forms of mange are transmissible to people.

AUTO-IMMUNE SKIN CONDITIONS

Auto-immune skin conditions are commonly referred to as being allergic to yourself. Allergies, though, usually result in inflammatory reactions to an outside stimulus. Auto-immune diseases cause serious damage to the tissues which are involved.

The best known auto-immune disease is lupus. It affects people as well as dogs. The symptoms are very variable and may affect the kidneys, bones, blood chemistry and skin. It can be fatal to both dogs and humans, though it is not thought to be transmissible. It is usually successfully treated with cortisone, prednisone or similar corticosteroid, but extensive use of these drugs can have harmful side effects.

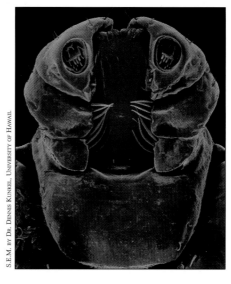

The head of the dog tick, *Dermacentor variabilis,* magnified about 90x.

S.E.M. BY DR. DENNIS KUNKEL, UNIVERSITY OF HAWAII.

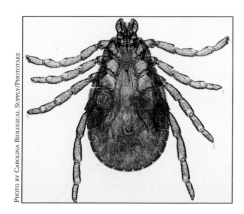

PHOTO BY CAROLINA BIOLOGICAL SUPPLY/PHOTOTAKE

sites live in peaceful cooperation with their hosts (symbiosis), while the dumb parasites kill their host. Most of the worm infections are relatively easy to control. If they are not controlled they eventually weaken the host dog to the point that other medical problems occur, but they are not dumb parasites.

A brown dog tick, *Rhipicephalus sanguineus.*

An uncommon dog tick of the genus *Ixode.* Magnified 10x.

INTERNAL PARASITES

Most animals—fishes, birds and mammals, including dogs and humans—have worms and other parasites which live inside their bodies. According to Dr. Herbert R. Axelrod, the fish pathologist, there are two kinds of parasites: dumb and smart. The smart para-

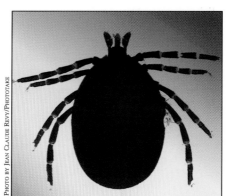

PHOTO BY JEAN CLAUDE REVY/PHOTOTAKE

131

ROUNDWORMS

The roundworms that infect dogs are scientifically known as *Toxocara canis*. They live in the dog's intestine. The worms shed eggs continually. It has been estimated that a Boxer produces about 150 grammes of faeces every day. Each gramme of faeces averages 10,000–12,000 eggs of roundworms. There are no known areas in which dogs roam that does not contain the eggs of roundworms. The greatest danger of roundworms is that they infect people, too! It is wise to have your dog tested regularly for roundworms.

Pigs also have roundworm infections which can be passed to human and dogs. The typical roundworm parasite is called *Ascaris lumbricoides*.

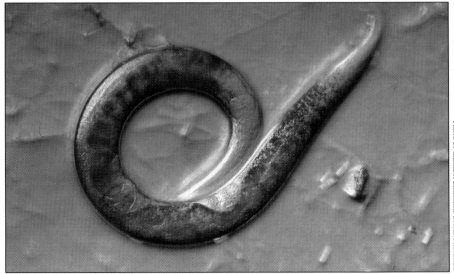

The roundworm, *Ascaris lumbricoides*, infects dogs and humans. Magnified about 175x.

PHOTO BY CAROLINA BIOLOGICAL SUPPLY/PHOTOTAKE

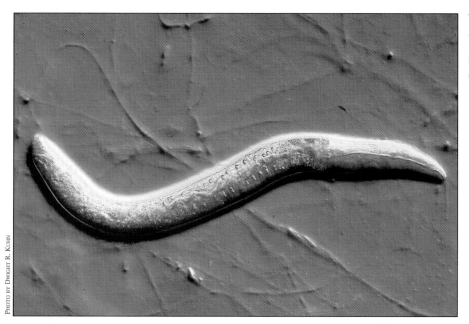

The roundworm, *Ascaris lumbricoides*, infects humans, dogs and pigs.

Photo by Dwight R. Kuhn

HOOKWORMS

The worm *Ancylostoma caninum* is commonly called the dog hookworm. It is dangerous to humans and cats. It also has teeth by which it attaches itself to the intestines of the dog. Because it changes the site of its attachment about six times a day, the dog loses blood from each detachment, possibly causing iron-deficiency anaemia. They are easily purged from the dog with many medications, the best of which seems to be ivermectin even though it has not been approved for such use.

TAPEWORMS

There are many species of tapeworms. They are carried by fleas! The dog eats the flea and thus starts the tapeworm cycle. Humans can also be infected with tapeworms, so don't eat fleas! Fleas are so small that your dog could pass them onto your hands, your plate or your food and thus make it possible for you to ingest a flea which is carrying tapeworm eggs.

While tapeworm infection is not life threatening in dogs (smart parasite!), it can be the cause of a very serious liver disease for humans. About 50 percent of the humans infected with Echinococcus multilocularis, causing alveolar hydatis, perish.

133

Male and female hookworms, *Ancylostoma caninum*, can infect Boxers.

The roundworm, *Rhabditis*.

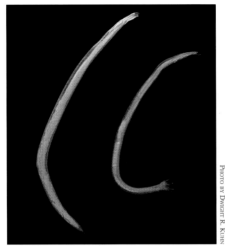

PHOTO BY DWIGHT R. KUHN

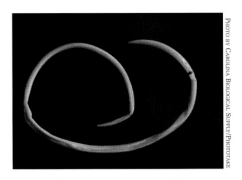

PHOTO BY CAROLINA BIOLOGICAL SUPPLY/PHOTOTAKE

DID YOU KNOW?

Humans, rats, squirrels, foxes, coyotes, wolves, mixed breeds of dogs and purebred dogs are all susceptible to tapeworm infection. Except for humans, tapeworms are usually not a fatal infection.

Infected individuals can harbour a thousand parasitic worms.

Tapeworms have two sexes—male and female (many other worms have only one sex—male and female in the same worm).

If dogs eat infected rats or mice, they get the tapeworm disease.

One month after attaching to a dog's intestine, the worm starts shedding eggs. These eggs are infective immediately.

Infective eggs can live for a few months without a host animal.

Roundworms, hookworms, whipworms and tapeworms are just a few of the commonly known worms which infect dogs.

HEARTWORMS

Heartworms are thin, extended worms up to 30 cms (12 ins.) long which live in a dog's heart and major blood vessels around the heart. Boxers may have to 200 of these worms. The symptoms may be loss of energy, loss of appetite, coughing, the development of a pot belly and anaemia.

Heartworms are transmitted by mosquitoes. The mosquito drinks the blood of an infected dog and takes in larvae with the blood. The larvae, called microfilaria, develop within the body of the mosquito and are passed on to the next dog bitten after the larvae mature. It takes two to three weeks for the larvae to develop to the infective stage within the body of the mosquito. Dogs should be treated at about six weeks of age, then every six months.

Blood testing for heartworms is not necessarily indicative of how seriously your dog is infected. This is a dangerous disease. Dogs in the United Kingdom are not affected by heartworm.

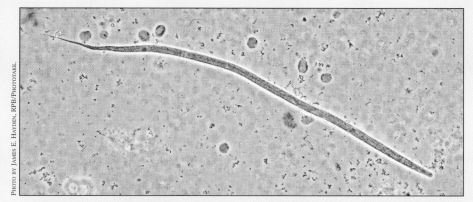

The heartworm, *Dirofilaria immitis.*

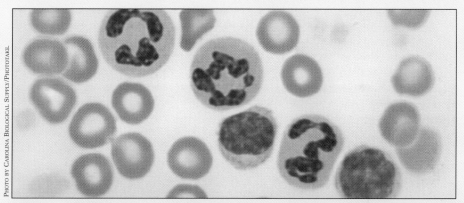

Magnified heartworm larvae, *Dirofilaria immitis.*

The heart of a dog infected with canine heartworm, *Dirofilaria immitis.*

 # First Aid
at a Glance

Burns
Place the affected area under cool water;
use ice if only a small area is burnt.

Bee/Insect bites
Apply ice to relieve swelling; antihista-
mine dosed properly.

Animal bites
Clean any bleeding area; apply pressure
until bleeding subsides; go to the vet.

Spider bites
Use cold compress and a pressurised
pack to inhibit venom's spreading.

Antifreeze poisoning
Immediately induce vomiting by using
hydrogen peroxide.

Fish hooks
Removal best handled by vet;
hook must be cut in order to remove.

Snake bites
Pack ice around bite; contact vet
quickly; identify snake for proper
antivenin.

Automobile accident
Move dog from roadway with blanket;
seek veterinary aid.

Shock
Calm the dog, keep him warm; seek
immediate veterinary help.

Nosebleed
Apply cold compress to the nose; apply
pressure to any visible abrasion.

Bleeding
Apply pressure above the area; treat
wound by applying a cotton pack.

Heat stroke
Submerge dog in cold bath; cool down
with fresh air and water; go to the vet.

Frostbite/Hypothermia
Warm the dog with a warm bath, electric
blankets or hot water bottles.

Abrasions
Clean the wound and wash out
thoroughly with fresh water;
apply antiseptic.

 *Remember: an injured dog may attempt
to bite a helping hand from fear and confusion.
Always muzzle the dog before trying to offer assistance.*

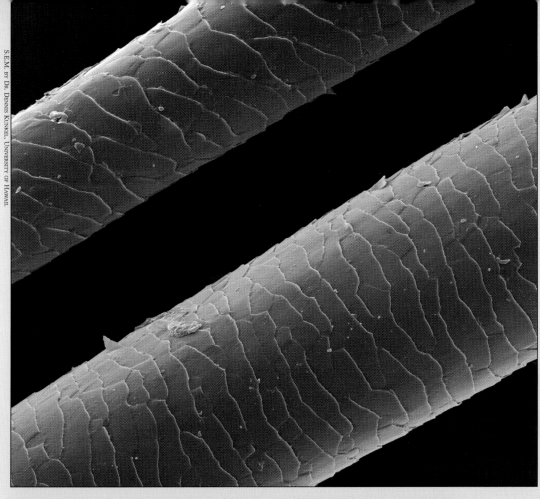

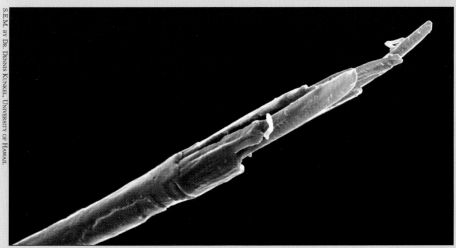

Normal, healthy Boxer hairs, above, as evidenced by the smooth cuticle, magnified at 500x. Left, the tip of a Boxer hair magnified 2,000x. Notice the split end. These revolutionary micrographs were taken specifically for this book by Dr. Dennis Kunkel at the University of Hawaii.

When Your Boxer Gets Old

The term *old* is a qualitative term. For dogs, as well as their masters, old is relative. Certainly we can all distinguish between a puppy Boxer and an adult Boxer—there are the obvious physical traits such as size and appearance, and personality traits like their antics and the expressions on their faces. Puppies that are nasty are very rare. Puppies and young dogs like to play with children. Children's natural exuberance is a good match for the seemingly endless energy of young dogs. They like to run, jump, chase and retrieve. When dogs grow up and cease their interaction with children, they are often thought of as being too old to play with the kids.

On the other hand, if a Boxer is only exposed to people over 60 years of age, its life will normally be less active and it will not seem to be getting old as soon as its activity level slows down.

If people live to be 100 years old, dogs live to be 20 years old. While this is a good rule of thumb, it is VERY inaccurate. When trying to compare dog years to human years, you cannot make a generalisation about all dogs. You can make the generalisation that, say, 11 years is a good life span for a Boxer, but you cannot compare it to that of a Chihuahua, as many small breeds typically live longer than large breeds. Dogs are generally considered mature within three years. They can reproduce even earlier. So the first three years of a dog's life are more like seven times that of comparable humans. That means a three-year-old dog is like a 21-year-old person. As the curve of comparison shows, there is no hard and fast

Older dogs still like to play and receive attention, but their physical abilities diminish as they are slowed down by age.

DID YOU KNOW?

An old dog starts to show one or more of the following symptoms:

• The hair on its face and paws starts to turn grey. The colour breakdown usually starts around the eyes and mouth.

• The exercise routine becomes more and more tedious and the dog almost refuses to join exercises that it previously enjoyed.

• Food intake diminishes.

• Responses to calls, whistles and other signals are ignored more and more.

• Eye contact indicates aloofness and does not evoke tail wagging (assuming they always did).

As grey begins to appear on the muzzle, old age starts to become evident.

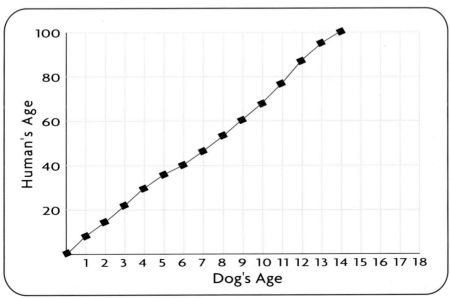

Older Boxers take more time in relieving themselves than younger dogs.

rule for comparing dog and human ages. The comparison is made even more difficult, for not all humans age at the same rate...and human females live longer than human males.

WHAT TO LOOK FOR IN SENIORS

Most veterinary surgeons and behaviourists use the seventh-year mark as the time to consider a dog a 'senior.' The term 'senior' does not imply that the dog is geriatric and has begun to fail in mind and body. Ageing is essentially a slowing process. Humans readily admit that they feel a difference in their activity level from age 20 to 30, and then from 30 to 40, etc. By treating the seven-year-old dog as a senior, owners are able to implement certain therapeutic and preventive medical strategies with the help of their veterinary surgeons. A senior-care programme should include at least two veterinary visits per year, screening sessions to determine the dog's health status, as well as nutritional counselling. Veterinary surgeons determine the senior dog's health status through a blood smear for a complete blood count, serum chemistry profile with electrolytes, urinalysis, blood pressure check, electrocardiogram, ocular tonometry (pressure on the eyeball), and dental prophylaxis.

Such an extensive programme for senior dogs is well advised before owners start to see the obvious physical signs of ageing, such as slower and inhibited movement, greying, increased sleep/nap periods, and disinterest in play and other activity. This preventative programme promises a longer, healthier life for the ageing dog. Amongst the physical problems common in ageing dogs are the loss of sight and vision, arthritis, kidney and liver failure, diabetes mellitus, heart disease, and Cushing's disease (a hormonal disease).

In addition to the physical manifestations discussed, there are some behavioural changes and problems related to ageing dogs. Dogs suffering from hearing or vision loss, dental discomfort or arthritis can become aggressive. Likewise the near-deaf and/or blind dog may be startled more easily and react in an unexpectedly aggressive manner. Seniors suffering from senility can become more impatient and irritable. Housesoiling accidents are associated with loss of mobility, kidney problems, loss of sphincter control as well as plaque accumula-

tion, physiological brain changes, and reactions to medications. Older dogs, just like young puppies, suffer from separation anxiety, which can lead to excessive barking, whining, housesoiling, and destructive behaviour. Seniors may become fearful of everyday sounds, such as vacuum cleaners, heaters, thunder, and passing traffic. Some dogs have difficulty sleeping, due to discomfort, the need for frequent potty visits, and the like. Owners should avoid spoiling the older dog with too many fatty treats. Obesity is a common problem in older dogs and subtracts years from their lifespan. Keep the senior dog as trim as possible since excessive weight puts additional stress on the body's vital organs. Some breeders recommend supplementing the diet with foods high in fibre and lower in calories. Adding fresh vegetables and

DID YOU KNOW?
The bottom line is simply that a dog is getting old when YOU think it is getting old because it slows down in its general activities, including walking, running, eating, jumping and retrieving. On the other hand, certain activities increase, like more sleeping, more licking your hands and body, more barking and more repetition of habits like going to the door when you put your coat on without being called.

Your aging Boxer deserves all the time and love you can devote to him.

marrow broth to the senior's diet makes a tasty, low-calorie, low-fat supplement. Vets also offer specialty diets for senior dogs that are worth exploring.

Your dog, as he nears his twilight years, needs his owner's patience and good care more than ever. Never punish an older dog for an accident or abnormal behaviour. For all the years of love, protection and companionship that your dog has provided, he deserves special attention and courtesies. The older dog may need to relieve himself at 3 a.m. because he can no longer hold it for eight hours. Older dogs may not be able to remain crated for more than two or three hours. It may be time to give up a sofa or chair to your old friend. Although he may not seem as enthusiastic about your attention and petting, he does appreciate the considerations you offer as he gets older.

Your Boxer does not understand why his world is slowing down. Owners must make the transition into the golden years as pleasant and rewarding as possible.

WHAT TO DO WHEN THE TIME COMES

You are never fully prepared to make a rational decision about putting your dog to sleep. It is very obvious that you love your Boxer or you would not be reading this book. Putting a loved dog to sleep is extremely difficult. It is a decision that must be made with your veterinary surgeon. You are usually forced to make the decision when one of the life-threatening symptoms listed above becomes serious enough for you to seek medical (veterinary) help.

If the prognosis of the malady indicates the end is near and your beloved pet will only suffer more and experience no enjoyment for the balance of its life, then there is no choice but euthanasia.

WHAT IS EUTHANASIA?

Euthanasia derives from the Greek meaning good death. In other words, it means the planned, painless killing of a dog suffering from a painful, incurable condition, or who is so aged that it cannot walk, see, eat or control its excretory functions.

Euthanasia is usually accomplished by injection with an overdose of an anaesthesia or barbiturate. Aside from the prick of the needle, the experience is painless.

HOW ABOUT YOU?

The days during which the dog becomes ill and the end occurs can be unusually stressful for you. If this is your first experience with the death of a loved one, you may need the comfort dictated by your religious beliefs. If you are the

CDS: COGNITIVE DYSFUNCTION SYNDROME
"Old Dog Syndrome"

There are many ways to evaluate old-dog syndrome. Veterinary surgeons have defined CDS (cognitive dysfunction syndrome) as the gradual deterioration of cognitive abilities. These are indicated by changes in the dog's behaviour. When a dog changes its routine response, and maladies have been eliminated as the cause of these behavioural changes, then CDS is the usual diagnosis.

More than half the dogs over 8 years old suffer some form of CDS. The older the dog, the more chance it has of suffering from CDS. In humans, doctors often dismiss the CDS behavioral changes as part of 'winding down.'

There are four major signs of CDS: frequent toilet accidents inside the home, sleeps much more or much less than normal, acts confused, and fails to respond to social stimuli.

SYMPTOMS OF CDS

FREQUENT TOILET ACCIDENTS
- *Urinates in the house.*
- *Defecates in the house.*
- *Doesn't signal that he wants to go out.*

SLEEP PATTERNS
- *Moves much more slowly.*
- *Sleeps more than normal during the day.*
- *Sleeps less during the night.*
- *Walks around listlessly and without a destination goal.*

CONFUSION
- *Goes outside and just stands there.*
- *Appears confused with a faraway look in his eyes.*
- *Hides more often.*
- *Doesn't recognise friends.*
- *Doesn't come when called.*

FAILS TO RESPOND TO SOCIAL STIMULI
- *Comes to people less frequently, whether called or not.*
- *Doesn't tolerate petting for more than a short time.*
- *Doesn't come to the door when you return home from work.*

head of the family and have children, you should have involved them in the decision of putting your Boxer to sleep. In any case, euthanasia alone is painful and stressful for the family of the dog. Unfortunately, it does not end there. The decision-making process is just as hard.

Usually your dog can be maintained on drugs for a few days while it is kept in the clinic in order to give you ample time to make a decision. During this time, talking with members of the family or religious representatives, or even people who have lived through this same experience, can ease the burden of your inevitable decision...but then what?

THE FINAL RESTING PLACE

Dogs can have the same privileges as humans. They can be buried in their entirety in a pet cemetery (very expensive) in a burial con-

Cemeteries for pets exist. Consult your veterinary surgeon to help you locate one.

DID YOU KNOW?
The more open discussion you have about the whole stressful occurrence, the easier it will be for you when the time comes.

tainer, buried in your garden in a place suitably marked with a stone or newly planted tree or bush, cremated with the ashes being given to you, or even stuffed and mounted by a taxidermist.

All of these options should be discussed frankly and openly with your veterinary surgeon. Do not be afraid to ask financial questions. Cremations are usually mass burning and the ashes you get may not be the ashes of your beloved dog. There are very small crematoriums available to all veterinary clinics. If you want a private cremation, your vet can usually arrange it. However, this may be a little more expensive.

Growing old together, these two senior citizens get along better than an older dog might get on with a younger one.

GETTING ANOTHER DOG?

The grief of losing your beloved dog will be as lasting as the grief of losing a human friend or relative. You cannot go out and buy another grandfather, but you can go out and buy another Boxer. In most cases, if your dog died of old age (if there is such a thing), it had slowed down considerably. Do you want a new Boxer puppy to replace it? Or are you better off in finding a more mature Boxer, say two to three years of age, which will usually be house-trained and will have an already developed personality.

The decision is, of course, your own. Do you want another Boxer? Perhaps you want a smaller or larger dog? How much do you want to spend on a dog? Whatever you decide, do it as quickly as possible. Most people usually buy the same breed they had before because they know (and love) the characteristics of that breed. Then, too, they often know people who have the same breed and perhaps they are lucky enough that one of their friends expects a litter soon. What could be better?

Showing Your Boxer

Is the Boxer puppy you selected growing into a flashy handsome representative of his breed? You are rightly proud of your handsome little tyke, and he has mastered nearly all of the basic obedience commands that you have taught him. How about attending a dog show and seeing how the other half of the dog-loving world lives! Even if you never imagined yourself standing in the centre ring at the Crufts Dog Show, why not dream a little?

The first concept that the canine novice learns when watching a dog show is that each breed first competes against members of its own breed. Once the judge has selected the best member of each breed, then that chosen dog will compete with other dogs in its group. Finally the best of each

With practice and patience, you can learn to handle and show your own Boxer. You will learn just how well your dog measures up to the Kennel Club's standard and how to show him to his best advantage.

group will compete for Best in Show and Reserve Best in Show.

The second concept that you must understand is that the dogs are not actually competing with one another. The judge compares

each dog against the breed standard, which is a written description of the ideal specimen of the breed. This imaginary dog never walked into a show ring, has never been bred and, to the woe of dog breeders around the globe, does

If you have a show-quality puppy, begin his show training by three months of age.

American Ch. Jacquet's Black Watch, Bill Scolnik's top-winning champion, is considered by many to be an exceptionally handsome dog. Breeder, Richard Tomita.

not exist. Breeders attempt to get as close to this ideal as possible, with every litter, but theoretically the 'perfect' dog is so elusive that it is impossible. (And if the 'perfect' dog were born, breeders and judges would never agree that it was indeed 'perfect.')

If you are interested in exploring dog shows, your best bet is to join your local breed club. These clubs host shows (often matches and open shows for beginners), send out newsletters, offer training days and provide an outlet to meet members who are often friendly and generous with their advice and contacts. To locate the nearest breed club for you, contact The Kennel Club, the ruling body for the British dog world, not just for conformation shows, but for work-ing trials, obedience trials, agility trials and field trials. The Kennel Club furnishes the rules and regulations for all these events plus general dog registration and other basic requirements of dog ownership. Its annual show, held in

English and American Ch. Jacquet's Dreams of Loriga, belonging to the Dotorovici family, is a truly magnificent specimen of the breed. Breeder, Richard Tomita.

includes Great Britain, Australia, South Africa and beyond, there are different kinds of shows. At the most competitive and prestigious of these shows, the Championship Shows, a dog can earn Challenge Certificates, and thereby become a 'champion.' A dog must earn three Challenge Certificates under three different judges to earn the prefix of 'Sh Ch.' or 'Ch.' Note that some breeds must qualify in a field trial in order to gain the title of full champion. Challenge Certificates are awarded to a very small percentage of the dogs competing, and the number of Challenge Certificates awarded in any one year is based upon the total number of dogs in each breed entered for competition. There are two types of Championship Shows, a general show, where all breeds recognised by The Kennel Club can enter, and a breed show, which is limited to only a single breed.

Birmingham, is the largest bench show in England. Every year no fewer than 20,000 of the U.K.'s best dogs qualify to participate in a marvelous show lasting four days.

In shows held under the auspices of The Kennel Club, which

The Kennel Club does not make CCs (or tickets) available to every breed at every show. This factor makes attaining a championshiup ever more challenging.

Open Shows are generally less competitive and are frequently used as 'practice shows' for young dogs. These

Besides the personal rewards of having a champion dog, there are plenty of trophies, ribbons and plaques.

shows, of which there are hundreds each year, can be invitingly social events and are great first show experiences for the novice. If you're just considering watching a show to wet your paws, an Open Show is a great choice.

While Championship and Open Shows are most important for the beginner to understand, there are other types of shows in which the interested dog owner can participate. Training clubs, for example, sponsor Matches that can be entered on the day of the show for a nominal fee. These introductory level exhibitions are uniquely run: two dogs are pulled from a raffle and 'matched,' the winner of that match goes on to the next round, and eventually only one dog is left undefeated.

Exemption shows are similar in that they are simply fun classes and usually held in conjunction with small agricultural shows. Primary shows can also be entered on the day of the event and dogs entered must not have won anything towards their titles. Sanction and Limited shows must be entered well in advance, and there are limitations upon who can enter. Regardless of which type show you choose to begin with, you and your dog will have a grand time competing and learning your way about the shows.

Before you actually step into the ring, you would be well

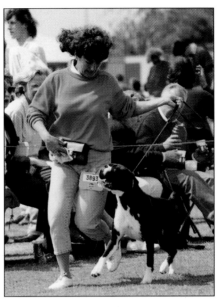

Showing your Boxer requires some physical exertion on your part. The Boxer's gait is important during its evaluation by the judges.

advised to sit back and observe the judge's ring procedure. If it is your first time in the ring, do not be over-anxious and run to the front of the line. It is much better when you can stand back and study how the exhibitor in front of you is performing. The judge asks each handler to

HOW TO ENTER A DOG SHOW
1. Obtain an entry form and show schedule from the Show Secretary.
2. Select the classes that you want to enter and complete the entry form.
3. Transfer your dog into your name at The Kennel Club. (Be sure that this matter is handled before entering.)
4. Find out how far in advance show entries must be made. Oftentimes it's more than a couple of months.

The famous Jacquet Boxer strain is known for its intelligence and sweet temperament as well as the wondrous expressions on the dogs' faces.

South African Ch. Osiris vom Okeler Forst illustrates a dog of slightly different appearance than European and American examples of the Boxer.

DID YOU KNOW?

You can get information about dog shows from kennel clubs and breed clubs:

Fédération Cynologique Internationale
14, rue Leopold II, B-6530 Thuin, Belgium

The Kennel Club
1-5 Clarges St., Piccadilly, London W1Y 8AB, UK
www.the-kennel-club.org.uk

American Kennel Club
5580 Centerview Dr., Raleigh, NC 27606-3390, USA
www.akc.org

Canadian Kennel Club
89 Skyway Ave., Suite 100, Etobicoke, Ontario
M9W 6R4 Canada
www.ckc.ca

'stand' the dog, hopefully showing the dog off to his best advantage. The judge will observe the dog from a distance and from different angles, approach the dog, check his teeth, overall structure, alertness and muscle tone, as well as consider how well the dog 'conforms' to the standard. Most importantly, the judge will have the exhibitor move the dog around the ring in some pattern that he or she should specify (another advantage to not going first, but always listen since some judges change their directions, and the judge is always right!) Finally the judge will give the dog one last look before moving on to the next exhibitor.

If you are not in the top three at your first show, do not be dis-

couraged. Be patient and consistent and you will eventually find yourself in the winning lineup. Remember that the winners were once in your shoes and have devoted many hours and much money to earn the placement. If you find that your dog is losing every time and never getting a nod, it may be time to consider a different dog sport or just to enjoy your Boxer as a pet.

WORKING TRIALS
Working trials can be entered by any well-trained dog of any breed, not just Gundogs or Working dogs. Many dogs that earn the Kennel Club Good Citizen Dog award choose to participate in a working trial. There are five stakes at both open and championship levels: Companion Dog (CD), Utility Dog (UD), Working Dog (WD), Tracking Dog (TD), and Patrol Dog (PD). Like in conformation shows, dogs compete against a standard and if the dog reaches the qualifying

TERMINOLOGY
IN GERMAN PEDIGREES

Fahrtenhund (FH): an advanced degree in tracking
Gekort: suitability for breeding
Gekort bis EzA: suitability for breeding for nine years in males, eight years in females
Internationale Prufungsordnung (IPO): international trials for tracking, obedience and protection
Körung: achievement of all requirements for breeding suitability, conformation, protection, excellent hips
Leistungszucht (LS): parents and grandparents have Schutzhund degrees and Körung
Schutzhund (SchH): working dog degree encompassing areas of tracking, obedience and protection
Sieger: male champion at a show
Siegerin: female champion at a show
Wachhund (WH): guard dog training (without bite work as in SchH)
Zuchttauglichkeitsprüfung (ZTPR): German breeding suitability test

Olimpio del Colle dell' Infinito, owned by Alessando Tanoni, is a wonderful example of the Italian-style Boxer.

Sadeo Kikuchi's Japanese Ch. Cherry Heim Bushu Jacquet, bred out of Rick Tomita's American exports.

Norwegian Ch. Astovega Opuntia, owned by Cecille Strømstad and Henning Lund.

Impala v. Okeler Forst, SchH 1, AD, a Best in Show winner owned by Ralf Brinkmann, Germany, holds the title of World One Year Old Champion.

Tenor de Loermo, owned by Ernesto Molins and Juan Barcelo in Valencia, Spain, earned the title of the 1994 World Champion European Young Dog.

Ch. Canara Coast Alaska, owned by Nita Dhar, Delhi, India, produced five champion offspring.

mark, it obtains a certificate. Divided into groups, each exercise must be achieved 70 percent in order to qualify. If the dog achieves 80 percent in the open level, it receives a Certificate of Merit (COM), in the championship level, it receives a Qualifying Certificate. At the CD stake, dogs must participate in four groups, Control, Stay, Agility and Search (Retrieve and Nosework). At the next three levels, UD, WD and TD, there are only three groups: Control, Agility and Nosework.

Agility consists of three jumps: a vertical scale, a six-foot wall of planks; a clear jump, a basic three-foot hurdle with a removable top bar; and a long jump of angled planks stretching nine feet.

To earn the UD, WD and TD, dogs must track approximately one-half mile for articles laid from one-half hour to three hours ago. Tracks consist of turns and legs, and fresh ground is used for each participant.

The fifth stake, PD, involves teaching manwork, which of course is not recommended for every breed.

FIELD TRIALS AND WORKING TESTS
Working tests are frequently used to prepare dogs for field trials, the purpose of which is to heighten the instincts and natural abilities of gundogs. Live game is not used

in working tests. Unlike field trials, working tests do not count toward a dog's record at the Kennel Club, though the same judges often oversee working tests. Field trials began in England in 1947, and are only moderately popular among dog folk. While breeders of Working and Gundog breeds concern themselves with the field abilities of their dogs, there is considerably less interest in field trials than dog shows. In order for dogs to become full champions, certain breeds must qualify in the field as well. Upon gaining three CCs in the show ring, the dog is designated a Show Champion (Sh Ch). The title Champion (Ch) requires that the dog gain an award at a field trial, be a 'special qualifier' at a field trial or pass a 'special show dog qualifier' judged by a field trial judge on a shooting day.

AGILITY TRIALS

Agility trials began in the United Kingdom in 1977 and have since spread around the world, especially to the United States, where they enjoy strong popularity. The handler directs his dog over an obstacle course that includes jumps (such as those used in the working trials), as well as tyres, the dog walk, weave poles, pipe tunnels, collapsed tunnels, etc. The Kennel Club requires that dogs not be trained for agility until they are 12 months old. This dog

The world's first long-tailed champion Boxer, Norwegian Ch. Boxerhavens Born for Adventure, is owned by Jorunn Selland. It seems quite unusual to see a Boxer with a natural tail.

Ch. Newlaithe Marietta, owned by Christine Beardsell of Huddersfield, England.

Newlaithe Tex Style at seven months of age is owned by Christine and Pat Beardsell. This is a typical high-quality British youngster.

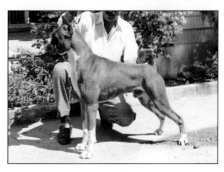

Indian Ch. Aryanoush's Vendetta was the Dog of the Year (All Breeds) in 1995 and the Top Boxer 1996 in India. Owned by N. Adil Mirza.

Your Boxer can be entered in many classes at many dog shows. Enter the class that suits you best.

English Ch. Newlaithe High Fashion has 'the perfect Boxer head in England,' so boasted owner Patrick Beardsell.

sport intends to be great fun for dog and owner and interested owners should join a training club that has obstacles and experienced agility handlers who can introduce you and your dog to the 'ropes' (and tyres, tunnels and so on).

FÉDÉRATION CYNOLOGIQUE INTERNATIONALE

Judges examine the Boxer's mouth to be sure that the bite is correct and that the teeth are present and in good condition.

Established in 1911, the Fédération Cynologique Internationale represents the 'world kennel club,' the international body brings uniformity to the breeding, judging and showing of purebred dogs. Although the FCI originally included only European nations, namely France, Holland, Austria and Belgium, the latter of which remains the headquarters, the organisation

today embraces nations on six continents and recognises well over 400 breeds of purebred dog. There are three titles attainable through the FCI: the International Champion, which is the most prestigious; the International Beauty Champion,

which is based on aptitude certificates in different countries; and the International Trial Champion, which is based on achievement in obedience trials in different countries. Of course, quarantine laws in England and Australia prohibit most exhibitors from entering FCI shows, though the rest of the European Union nations do participate in these impressive canine spectacles, the largest of which is the World Dog Show, hosted in a different country each year. FCI sponsors both national and international shows. The hosting country determines the judging system and breed standards are always based on the breed's country of origin.

The Kennel Club's *Good Citizen Dog Scheme* exercises are a wonderful experience for both you and your dog. This photo was taken at the world famous Crufts Dog Show.

English Ch. Mitchum of Sunhawk Norwatch with two of his puppies. Owned by Robert Tyrrell and Hilda and Peter Foster of Australia.

CLASSES AT DOG SHOWS

There can be as many as 18 classes per sex for your breed. Check the show schedule carefully to make sure that you have entered your dog in the appropriate class. Among the classes offered can be: Minor Puppy (ages 6 to 9 months); Puppy (ages 6 to 12 months); Junior (ages 6 to 18 months); Beginners (handler or dog never won first place); as well as the following, each of which is defined in the schedule: Maiden; Novice; Tyro; Debutant; Undergraduate; Graduate; Postgraduate; Minor Limit; Mid Limit; Limit; Open; Veteran; Stud Dog; Brood Bitch; Progeny; Brace; and Team.

Understanding Your Dog's Behaviour

As a Boxer owner, you have selected your dog so that you and your loved ones can have a companion, a protector, a friend and a four-legged family member. You invest time, money and effort to care for and train the family's new charge. Of course, this chosen canine behaves perfectly! Well, perfectly like a dog.

THINK LIKE A DOG

Dogs do not think like humans, nor do humans think like dogs, though we try. Unfortunately, a dog is incapable of figuring out how humans think, so the responsibility falls on the owner to adopt a proper canine mind-set. Dogs cannot rationalise, and dogs exist in the present

Ch. Braia di Valdemone, owned by Ottavio and Isabella Perricone of Italy.

moment. Many dog owners make the mistake in training of thinking that they can reprimand their dog for something he did a while ago. Basically, you cannot even

You cannot reprimand a dog unless you catch him in the act.

reprimand a dog for something he did 20 seconds ago! Either catch him in the act or forget it! It is a waste of your and your dog's time—in his mind, you are reprimanding him for whatever he is doing at that moment.

The following behavioural problems represent some which owners most commonly encounter. Every dog is unique

and every situation is unique. No author could purport to solve your Boxer's problem simply by reading a script. Here we outline some basic 'dogspeak' so that owners' chances of solving behavioural problems are increased. Discuss bad habits with your veterinary surgeon and he/she can recommend a behavioural specialist to consult in appropriate cases. Since behavioural abnormalities are the leading reason owners abandon their pets, we hope that you will make a valiant effort to solve your Boxer's problem. Patience and understanding are virtues that dwell in every pet-loving household.

AGGRESSION

Aggression can be a very big problem in dogs, especially big dogs. Aggression, when not con-

Training a Boxer in Schutzhund is a way to channel his natural protective instincts.

trolled, becomes dangerous. An aggressive dog, no matter the size, may lunge at, bite or even attack a person or another dog. Aggressive behaviour is not to be tolerated. It is more than just inappropriate behaviour; it is not safe, especially with a large, powerful breed such as the Boxer. It is painful for a family to watch their dog become unpredictable in his behaviour to the point where they are afraid of the dog. And while not all aggressive behaviour is dangerous, it can be frightening: growling, baring teeth, etc. It is important to get to the root of the problem to ascertain why the dog is acting in this manner. Aggression is a display of dominance, and the dog should not have the dominant role in its pack, which is, in this case, your family.

It is important not to challenge an aggressive dog as this could provoke an attack. Observe your Boxer's body language. Does he make direct eye contact and stare? Does he try to make himself as large as possible: ears pricked, chest out, tail erect? Height and size signify authority in a dog pack—being taller or 'above' another dog literally means that he is 'above' in the social status. These body signals tell you that your Boxer thinks he is in charge, a prob-

At the famous ATIBOX show in Germany, the handlers allow the Boxers to square off so that the judges can evaluate the dog's courage and undaunted spirit.

If a Boxer will not stare straight into your eyes, you will probably have trouble training him.

lem that needs to be dealt with. An aggressive dog is unpredictable in that you never know when he is going to strike and what he is going to do. You cannot understand why a dog that

Boxers have expressive body language, though some aggressive Boxers are unpredictable.

is playful and loving one minute is growling and snapping the next.

The best solution is to consult a behavioural specialist, one who has experience with the Boxer if possible. Together, perhaps you can pinpoint the cause of your dog's aggression and do something about it. An aggressive dog cannot be trusted, and a dog that cannot be trusted is not safe to have as a family pet. If the pet Boxer becomes untrustworthy, he cannot be kept in the home with

the family. The family must get rid of the dog. In the worst case, the dog must be euthanised.

AGGRESSION TOWARD OTHER DOGS

A dog's aggressive behaviour toward another dog stems from not enough exposure to other dogs at an early age. If other dogs make your Boxer nervous and agitated, he will lash out as a protective mechanism. A dog who has not received sufficient exposure to other canines tends to believe that he is the only dog on the planet. The animal becomes so dominant that he does not even show signs that he is fearful or threatened. Without growling or any other physical signal as a warning, he will lunge at and bite the other dog. A way to correct this is to let your Boxer approach another dog when walking on lead. Watch very closely and at the very first sign of aggression, correct your Boxer and pull him away. Scold him for any sign of discomfort, and then praise him when he ignores or tolerates the other dog. Keep this up until either he stops the aggressive behaviour, learns to ignore the other dog or even accepts other dogs. Praise him lavishly for his correct behaviour.

DOMINANT AGGRESSION

A social hierarchy is firmly established in a wild dog pack.

Recognising all of the Boxer's moods helps the te the dog's steadiness and reliability.

Dog shows are terrific places for dogs to get to know one another. Introductions should only be made between dogs that are on leads and can be controlled.

The dog wants to dominate those under him and please those above him. Dogs know that there must be a leader. If you are not the obvious choice for emperor, the dog will assume the throne! These conflicting innate desires are what a dog owner is up against when he sets about training a dog. In training a dog to obey commands, the owner is reinforcing that he is the top dog in the 'pack' and that the dog should, and should want to, serve his superior. Thus, the owner is suppressing the dog's urge to dominate by modifying his behaviour and making him obedient.

An important part of training is taking every opportunity to reinforce that you are the leader. The simple action of making your Boxer sit to wait for his food instead of allowing him to

Older larger dogs are always in charge. Even this puppy knows how to concede to authority.

run up to get it when he wants it says that you control when he eats; he is dependent on you for food. Although it may be difficult, do not give in to your dog's wishes every time he whines at you or looks at you with pleading eyes. It is a constant effort to show the dog that his place in the pack is at the bottom. This is not meant to sound cruel or inhumane. You love your Boxer and you should treat him with care and affection. You (hopefully) did not get a dog just so you could boss around another creature. Dog training is not about being cruel or feeling important, it is about moulding the dog's behaviour into what is accept-

able and teaching him to live by your rules. In theory, it is quite simple: catch him in appropriate behaviour and reward him for it. Add a dog into the equation and it becomes a bit more trying, but as a rule of thumb, positive reinforcement is what works best.

With a dominant dog, punishment and negative reinforcement can have the opposite effect of what you are after. It can make a dog fearful and/or act out aggressively if he feels he is being challenged. Remember, a dominant dog perceives himself at the top of the social heap, and will fight to defend his perceived status. The best way to prevent that is to never give him

A tug of war with a stranger can become dangerous if the dog is aggressive.

When two dogs meet, dominance is always on display with specific body language.

ting, and praise him when he behaves properly. You are focusing on praise and on modifying his behaviour by rewarding him when he acts appropriately. By being gentle and by supervising his interactions, you are showing him that there is no need to be afraid or defensive.

SEXUAL BEHAVIOUR

Dogs exhibit certain sexual behaviours that may have influenced your choice of male or female when you first purchased your Boxer. Spaying/neutering will eliminate these behaviours, but if you are purchasing a dog that you wish to breed, you should be aware of what you will have to deal with throughout the dog's life.

reason to think that he is in control in the first place. If you are having trouble training your Boxer and it seems as if he is constantly challenging your authority, seek the help of an obedience trainer or behavioural specialist. A professional will work with both you and your dog to teach you effective techniques to use at home. Beware of trainers who rely on excessively harsh methods; scolding is necessary now and then, but the focus in your training should always be on positive reinforcement.

If you can isolate what brings out the fear reaction, you can help the dog get over it. Supervise your Boxer's interactions with people and other dogs, and praise the dog when it goes well. If he starts to act aggressively in a situation, correct him and remove him from the situation. Do not let people approach the dog and start petting him without your express permission. That way, you can have the dog sit to accept pet-

If your Boxer repeatedly challenges your authority, seek professional help.

Female dogs usually have two oestruses per year, each season lasting about three weeks. These are the only times in which a female dog will mate, and she usually will not allow this until the second week of the cycle. If a bitch is not bred during the heat cycle, it is not uncommon for her to experience a false pregnancy, in which her mammary glands swell and she exhibits maternal tendencies toward toys or other objects.

Owners must further recognise that mounting is not merely a sexual expression but also one of dominance. Be consistent and persistent and you will find that you can 'move mounters.'

CHEWING

The national canine pastime is chewing! Every dog loves to sink his 'canines' into a tasty bone, but sometimes that bone is attached to his owner's hand! Dogs need to chew, to massage their gums, to make their new teeth feel better and to exercise their jaws. This is a natural behaviour deeply imbedded in all things canine. Our role as owners is not to stop chewing, but to redirect it to positive, chew-worthy objects. Be an informed owner and purchase proper chew toys for your Boxer, like strong nylon bones made for large dogs. Be sure that the devices are safe and durable, since your dog's safety is at risk. Again, the owner is responsible for ensuring a dog-proof environment. The best answer is prevention: that is, put your shoes, handbags and other tasty objects in their proper places (out of the reach of the growing canine mouth). Direct puppies to their toys whenever you see them tasting the furniture legs or your pant leg. Make a loud noise to attract the pup's attention and immediately escort him to his chew toy and engage him with the toy for at least four minutes, praising and encouraging him all the while.

Some trainers recommend deterrents, such as hot pepper or another bitter spice or a product designed for this purpose, to discourage the dog from chewing on unwanted objects. This is sometimes reliable, though not as often as the manufacturers of such products claim. Test out the product with your own dog before investing in a case of it.

JUMPING UP

Jumping up is a dog's friendly way of saying hello! Some dog owners do not mind when their dog jumps up, which is fine for them. The problem arises when guests come to the house and the dog greets them in the same manner—whether they like it or not! However

Pick a command such as 'off' (avoid using 'down' since you will use that for the dog to lie down) and tell him 'off' when he jumps up. Place him on the ground on all fours and have him sit, praising him the whole time. Always lavish him with praise and petting when he is in the 'sit' position. That way you

Your Boxer puppy must be supplied with something safe to chew for the proper development of its teeth, gums and jaws.

friendly the greeting may be, chances are your visitors will not appreciate nearly being knocked over by 30 kgs. of Boxer. The dog will not be able to distinguish upon whom he can jump and whom he cannot. Therefore, it is probably best to discourage this behaviour entirely.

are still giving him a warm affectionate greeting, because you are as excited to see him as he is to see you!

DIGGING

Digging, which is seen as a destructive behaviour to humans, is actually quite a natural behaviour in dogs. Whether

There is nothing more frightening for your guest than to have your Boxer jump onto her. Your Boxer must be trained not to jump.

or not your dog is one of the 'earth dogs' (also known as terriers), his desire to dig can be irrepressible and most frustrating to his owners. When digging occurs in your garden, it is actually a normal behaviour redirected into something the dog can do in his everyday life. For example, in the wild a dog would be actively seeking food, making his own shelter, etc. He would be using his paws in a purposeful manner; he would be using them for his survival. Since you provide him with food and shelter, he has no need to use his paws for these purposes, and so the energy that he would be using manifests itself in the

form of little holes all over your garden and flower beds.

Perhaps your dog is digging as a reaction to boredom—it is somewhat similar to someone eating a whole bag of pretzels in front of the Tele—because they are there and there is not anything better to do! Basically, the answer is to provide the dog with adequate play and exercise so that his mind and paws are occupied, and so that he feels as if he is doing something useful.

Of course, digging is easiest to control if it is stopped as soon as possible, but it is often hard to catch a dog in the act, especially if he is alone in the garden during the day. If your dog is a compulsive digger and is not easily distracted by other activities, you can designate an area on your property where it is okay for him to dig. If you catch him digging in an off-limits area of the garden, immediately bring him to the approved area and praise him for digging there. Keep a close eye on him so that you can catch him, that is the only way he is going to understand what is permitted and what is not. If you bring him to a hole he dug an hour ago and tell him 'No,' he will understand that you are not fond of holes, or dirt, or flowers. If you catch him while he is stifle-deep in your tulips, that is when he will get your message.

BARKING

Dogs cannot talk—oh, what they would say if they could! Instead, barking is a dog's way of 'talking.' It can be somewhat frustrating because it is not always easy to tell what a dog means by his bark—is he excited, happy, frightened, angry? Whatever it is that the dog is trying to say, he should not be punished for barking. It is only when the barking becomes excessive, and when the excessive barking becomes a bad habit, does the behaviour need to be modified. If an intruder came into your home in the middle of the night and the dog barked a warning, wouldn't you be pleased? You would probably deem your dog a hero, a wonderful guardian and protector of the home. On the other hand, if a friend drops by unexpectedly and rings the doorbell and is greeted with a sudden sharp bark, you would probably be annoyed at the dog. But isn't it

just the same behaviour? The dog does not know any better…unless he sees who is at the door and it is someone he is familiar with, he will bark as a means of vocalising that his (and your) territory is being threatened. While your friend is not posing a threat, it is all the same to the dog. Barking is his means of letting you know that there is an intrusion, whether friend or foe, on your property. This type of barking is instinctive and should not be discouraged.

Excessive habitual barking, however, is a problem that should be corrected early on. As your Boxer grows up, you will be able to tell when his barking is purposeful and when it is for

Puppies feuding over a pedigree?

no reason. You will become able to distinguish your dog's different barks and with what they are associated. For example, the bark when someone comes to the door will be different from the bark when he is excited to see you. It is similar to a person's tone of voice, except that the dog has to rely totally on tone of voice because he does not have

Dogs like to dig in flower beds because the soil is usually soft. Correct your Boxer if you catch him digging. If you do not catch him in the act, wait until a better opportunity to correct him.

This little food thief wants to try an adult diet!

the benefit of using words. An incessant barker will be evident at an early age.

There are some things that encourage a dog to bark. For example, if your dog barks non-stop for a few minutes and you give him a treat to quiet him, he believes that you are rewarding him for barking. He will associate barking with getting a treat, and will keep doing it until he is rewarded.

FOOD STEALING

Is your dog devising ways of stealing food from your counter tops? If so, you must answer the following questions: Is your Boxer hungry, or is he 'constantly famished' like every other chow hound? Why is there food on the counter top? Face it, some dogs are more food-motivated than others; some dogs are total-

Feed a dog in its bowl— never from the table.

ly obsessed by a slab of brisket and can only think of their next meal. Food stealing is terrific fun and always yields a great reward—FOOD, glorious food.

The owner's goal, therefore, is to make the 'reward' less

rewarding, even startling! Plant a shaker can (an empty pop can with coins inside) on the counter so that it catches your pooch off-guard. There are other devices available that will surprise the dog when he is looking for a mid-afternoon snack. Such remote-control devices, though not the first choice of some trainers, allow the correction to come from the object instead of the owner. These devices are also useful to keep the snacking hound from napping on furniture that is forbidden.

BEGGING

Just like food stealing, begging is a favourite pastime of hungry puppies! With that same reward—FOOD! Dogs quickly learn that their owners keep the 'good food' for themselves, and that we humans do not dine on kibble alone. Begging is a conditioned response related to a specific stimulus, time and place. The sounds of the kitchen, cans and bottles opening, crinkling bags, the smell of food in preparation, etc., will excite the chow hound and soon the paws are in the air!

Here is the solution to stopping this behaviour: Never give into a beggar! You are rewarding the dog for sitting pretty, jumping up, whining and rubbing his nose into you by giving him that glorious reward—food. By ignoring the

dog, you will (eventually) force the behaviour into extinction. Note that the behaviour likely gets worse before it disappears, so be sure there are not any 'softies' in the family who will give in to little 'Oliver' every time he whimpers, 'More, please.'

Puppies often develop separation anxiety, which is really a fear of being alone.

SEPARATION ANXIETY

Puppies first experience separation anxiety, that is fear of being left alone, as soon as they are weaned and removed from their dam. This is a normal reaction, no different than the child who cries as his mum leaves him on the first day of school. Don't be like your sappy mum and cry right back—move on, and your Boxer puppy will suffer less in the long run.

Your Boxer may howl, whine or otherwise vocalise his displeasure at your leaving the house and his being left alone. This is a normal case of separation anxiety, but there are things that can be done to eliminate this problem. Your dog needs to learn that he will be fine on his own for a while and that he will not wither away if he is not attended to every minute of the day. In fact, constant attention can lead to separation anxiety in the first place. If you are endlessly coddling and cooing over your dog, he will come to expect this

You must control when the dog can eat. Do not give in to the begging-barking behaviour.

from you all of the time and it will be more traumatic for him when you are not there. Obviously, you enjoy spending time with your dog, and he thrives on your love and attention. However, it should not become a dependent relationship where he is heartbroken without you.

One thing you can do to minimise separation anxiety is to make your entrances and exits as low-key as possible. Do not give your dog a long drawn-out good-

> **DID YOU KNOW?**
> The number of dogs who suffer from separation anxiety is on the rise as more and more pet owners find themselves at work all day. New attention is being paid to this problem, which is especially hard to diagnose since it is only evident when the dog is alone. Research is currently being done to help educate dog owners about separation anxiety and about how they can help minimise this problem in their dogs.

bye, and do not lavish him with hugs and kisses when you return. This is giving in to the attention that he craves, and it will only make him miss it more when you are away. Another thing you can try is to give your dog a treat when you leave; this will not only keep him occupied and keep his mind off the fact

that you just left, but it will also help him associate your leaving with a pleasant experience.

You may have to accustom your dog to being left alone in intervals, much like when you introduced your pup to his crate. Of course, when your dog starts whimpering as you approach the door, your first instinct will be to run to him and comfort him, but do not do it! Really—eventually he will adjust and be just fine if you take it in small steps. His anxiety stems from being placed in an unfamiliar situation; by familiarising him with being alone he will learn that he is okay. That is not to say you should purposely leave your dog home alone, but the dog needs to know that while he can depend on you for his care, you do not have to be by his side 24 hours a day.

When the dog is alone in the house, he should be confined to his crate or a designated dog-proof area of the house. This should be the area in which he sleeps, so he should already feel comfortable there and this should make him feel more at ease when he is alone. This is just one of the many examples in which a crate is an invaluable tool for you and your dog, and another reinforcement of why your dog should view his crate as a 'happy' place, a place of his own.

COPROPHAGIA

Faeces eating is, to most humans, one of the most disgusting behaviours that their dog could engage in, yet to the dog it is perfectly normal. It is hard for us to understand why a dog would want to eat its own faeces; he could be seeking certain nutrients that are missing from his diet, he could be just plain hungry, or he could be attracted by the pleasing (to a dog) scent. While coprophagia most often refers to the dog eating his own faeces, a dog may likely eat that of another animal as well if he comes across it. Vets have found that diets with a low digestibility, containing relatively low levels of fibre and high levels of starch, increase coprophagia. Therefore, high-fibre diets may decrease the likelihood of dogs eating faeces. Both the consistency of the stool (how firm it feels in the dog's mouth) and the presence of undigested nutrients increase the likelihood. Dogs often find the stool of cats and horses more palatable than that of other dogs. Once the dog develops diarrhoea from faeces eating, it will likely quit this distasteful habit, since dogs tend to prefer eating harder faeces.

To discourage this behaviour, first make sure that the food you are feeding your dog is nutritionally complete and that he is getting enough food. If changes in his diet do not seem to work, and no medical cause can be found, you will have to modify the behaviour through environmental control before it becomes a habit. There are some tricks you can try, such as adding an unpleasant-tasting substance to

Keeping more than one puppy usually eases separation anxiety.

the faeces to make them unpalatable or adding something to the dog's food which will make it unpleasant tasting after it passes through the dog. The best way to prevent your dog from eating his stool is to make it unavailable—clean up after he eliminates and remove any stool from the garden. If it is not there, he cannot eat it.

Never reprimand the dog for stool eating, as this rarely impresses the dog. Vets recommend distracting the dog while he is in the act of stool eating. Another option is to muzzle the dog when he is in the garden to relieve himself; this usually is effective within 30 to 60 days. Coprophagia most frequently is seen in pups 6 to 12 months of age, and usually disappears around the dog's first birthday.

My Boxer

PUT YOUR PUPPY'S FIRST PICTURE HERE

Dog's Name _____

Date _____ Photographer _____